BREAKING
THE
PATTERNS
THAT
BREAK
YOU

BREAKING THE PATTERNS THAT BREAK YOU

HEALING FROM THE PAIN OF YOUR PAST AND FINDING REAL HOPE THAT LASTS

TORI HOPE PETERSEN

NELSON BOOKS

An Imprint of Thomas Nelson

Published in Nashville, Tennessee, by Nelson Books, an imprint of Thomas Nelson. Nelson Books and Thomas Nelson are registered trademarks of HarperCollins Christian Publishing, Inc.

Published in association with the literary agency of Wolgemuth & Wilson.

Thomas Nelson titles may be purchased in bulk for educational, business, fundraising, or sales promotional use. For information, please email SpecialMarkets@ ThomasNelson.com.

Unless otherwise noted, Scripture quotations are taken from The Holy Bible, New International Version®, NIV®. Copyright © 1973, 1978, 1984, 2011 by Biblica, Inc.® Used by permission of Zondervan. All rights reserved worldwide. www.Zondervan. com. The "NIV" and "New International Version" are trademarks registered in the United States Patent and Trademark Office by Biblica, Inc.®

Scripture quotations marked CSB® are taken from the Christian Standard Bible®. Copyright © 2017 by Holman Bible Publishers. Used by permission. Christian Standard Bible® and CSB® are federally registered trademarks of Holman Bible Publishers.

Scripture quotations marked ESV are taken from the ESV® Bible (The Holy Bible, English Standard Version®). Copyright © 2001 by Crossway, a publishing ministry of Good News Publishers. Used by permission. All rights reserved.

Scripture quotations marked GNT are taken from the Good News Translation® in Today's English Version—Second Edition. Copyright © 1992 American Bible Society. Used by permission. All rights reserved.

Scripture quotations marked NCV are taken from the New Century Version®. Copyright © 2005 by Thomas Nelson. Used by permission. All rights reserved.

Scripture quotations marked NLT are taken from the Holy Bible, New Living Translation. Copyright © 1996, 2004, 2015 by Tyndale House Foundation. Used by permission of Tyndale House Publishers, Inc., Carol Stream, Illinois 60188. All rights reserved.

Scripture quotations marked TPT are taken from The Passion Translation®. Copyright © 2017, 2018, 2020 by Passion & Fire Ministries, Inc. Used by permission. All rights reserved. ThePassionTranslation.com.

Names and identifying characteristics of some individuals have been changed to preserve their privacy.

ISBN 978-1-4002-5004-2 (TP)
ISBN 978-1-4002-5005-9 (ePub)

Library of Congress Control Number: 2024034319

Printed in the United States of America

24 25 26 27 28 LBC 5 4 3 2 1

To my husband, Jacob. I am more of who God has called me to be because of who you are in my life. Thanks for breaking patterns and healing alongside me. I love you, always.

To my children, Leyonder, Ezzeri, Sar, and Lorelei. God gave me a vision of you when I was just thirteen. Ever since, I've been aiming to live a life that would ensure you have what I did not—safety and love. In this pursuit, I found safety and true love in our heavenly Father. My hope is that as you get older and can read and understand these words, you, too, would fall madly in love with God, who is madly in love with you. My prayer is that you would soak in God's Word and allow it to help you see yourself through his eyes. I cherish you, and I marvel at the idea that God cherishes you so much more.

Imagine yourself as a living house. God comes in to rebuild that house. At first, perhaps, you can understand what He is doing. He is getting the drains right and stopping the leaks in the roof and so on: you knew that those jobs needed doing and so you are not surprised. But presently He starts knocking the house about in a way that hurts abominably and does not seem to make any sense. What on earth is He up to? The explanation is that He is building quite a different house from the one you thought of—throwing out a new wing here, putting on an extra floor there, running up towers, making courtyards. You thought you were being made into a decent little cottage: but He is building a palace. He intends to come and live in it Himself.

—C. S. LEWIS

CONTENTS

FOREWORD

By Bob Goff

WE ALL WANT TO LIVE BEAUTIFUL, MEANINGFUL LIVES. When Sweet Maria and I got married we set out to create a different life than the ones we had growing up. As my friend Tori says it, we were trying to "break the patterns" in our lives that have not served us well. Perhaps a few of those patterns in your life come to mind as you reflect on this idea.

At our wedding, the pastor told Sweet Maria and me that the two of us would become one. Early on in our marriage, I wanted Sweet Maria to be a lot like me and not surprisingly, Maria wanted me to be a lot like her. I have come to realize that our power lies in becoming more like who God meant for us to be. He isn't hoping that we will become better versions of ourselves, but more accurate reflections of him in the world. Tori's hope in writing these pages is that you will take a fresh look at yourself and delight in who you have been made to be and clear that path for the next version of you to thrive.

Through her honest and vulnerable stories, Tori taps us gently on the shoulder and reminds us the work of replacing threadbare and unwelcome patterns with beautiful and meaningful new ones is worth the effort.

At times it becomes hard to be honest with ourselves and see who we really are because we are indeed many things all at once. Some people experience me as the happy and fun balloon guy and they assume I don't have anything but happy, fun, helium-filled days. But sometimes I feel sad and punishingly lonely. This book reminds us there is room for a wide range of emotions and that if experiencing acceptance has cost us who we are, then that price has been too high. This book is your invitation to return to God and to the many good things you already are.

Perhaps you have been giving too much airtime to the opinions of others or have grown weary of maintaining a facade that does not reflect who you really are. These pages are your permission slip to return to yourself once again and delight in what might be possible once you get real with who are you are and your massive possibilities. My hope is that you will be reminded once again that God has a nickname for you and it is this: *beloved.* To live fully into the truth of this, you may need to make some gentle adjustments, not because you need fixing but because you are worthy of the name. I know you'll enjoy these pages as Tori leads you through the journey of finding healing and hope.

INTRODUCTION

Safe House

NEARLY THREE YEARS AGO, ABOUT FOUR YEARS INTO our marriage, my husband and I were excited to move back to my hometown. As we prepared to sell our home in Minnesota and purchase another in Ohio, we started house hunting. We both had things we wanted. I wanted a minimum of four bedrooms, so we could have a guest bedroom for hosting. Jacob wanted a multifamily house as an investment, so we could live in one side and rent out the other. I wanted a house that was move-in ready. Jacob wanted a house he could flip, renovate, and do projects in. It seemed like if neither of us compromised, we wouldn't find a home at all. But to our surprise, the hunt did not last long.

The second house we walked through was a hundred-year-old duplex. We ogled over the big wooden beams on the ceiling and the original wood floors. Each side of the duplex had four bedrooms, which was rare for a duplex. It was move-in ready *enough*, yet it had plenty of restoration projects for Jacob to tackle.

The house had been on the market for nearly a year because of the work that had to be done, so our Realtor was shocked when we put an offer on the house right after our ten-minute tour. The Realtor was even more surprised when we bought the home without an inspection and moved in just weeks later.

The truth is, we were running away from a painful place. And it's been Jacob's dream since we married to restore something as big and broken as our duplex. That home became our soft-landing pad, where we could make beautiful what had been broken in the home and in our hearts.

Months later, we signed up to volunteer at our church, where they required members to take a "spiritual gifts" assessment before determining how they should serve. Jacob and I tested highest for the same gift: hospitality. This wasn't a great surprise to me but a reminder of what has always brought us together: welcoming people in.

I feed people. He creates spaces. He collects chairs. I gather people to sit in them. I tell stories. He listens. I make spaces more beautiful. He makes the beautiful more useful. He's unfazed by broken buildings. I'm unafraid of the broken-hearted. Together, we hope to create safe places for the people who might need them, just as we have needed them ourselves.

Homemaking has never been my aspiration but making a

safe house has. I do not want to just manage a house. I want to create a home where anyone feels welcome and safe—a place where there is abundant food to eat, peace to sleep, and freedom to hurt. I want to create a safe house. I want to *be* a safe house.

But in a home that has been overused and unkept, where the foundation has been hit by sledgehammers of hateful words and walls have been torn down by hands that should have built them up, debris has to be moved out. Old walls need to be repaired. The foundation has to be rebuilt.

This is true about making a safe house out of a home, as much as it is true about making a safe house out of me and you.

While Jacob and I were restoring this hundred-year-old home, we would tackle one project only to witness it turn into ten new ones. Every broken thing revealed to us more broken things. Every small fix turned into more small fixes. I have found that it is the same for the problems, aches, and pains within ourselves.

But old homes possess the kind of beauty that is nearly impossible to build into new ones. Despite all its brokenness, we would never tear the entire building down. The same is true for you and me; because we have survived a great deal, we should commend ourselves for how far we have gotten and how far we plan to go. What little Tori and little you survived is admirable, and we aren't trying to get rid of our past selves. However, as houses age, we must change the way we care for them; and since time has gone on, we, too, should take a look into ourselves to see what patterns our little selves might have acquired that don't quite work for us anymore.

My hope is that we might tear down lies that have lived freely in our hearts and minds for far too long. Then, together, we can replace them with truth. My hope is that we identify what is no longer holding us up and replace it with a stronger, longer-lasting foundation. In the end we will have built a safe house out of ourselves.

I wrote most of my debut memoir, *Fostered*, at the age of twenty-three. The book was published when I was twenty-six. While I was warned that publishing a memoir at such a young age came with the risk of scrutiny and judgment, I did not fully understand how it would feel when *I* changed but my book remained the same.

The memoir will include the same words and stories forever. That's the risk writers and artists take when we put our work into the world—as we evolve, our past work remains stagnant. That said, I've chosen to write this book knowing I'll likely look back at some words, someday, with a changed mind. But I believe this book will do what the first one did: meet people where they are, especially as they heal. Honest and raw storytelling may be the greatest power we have. I continue writing because I have more good reasons to "tell" than I have reasons not to.

My first book is what I would call a mountaintop book. It illustrated the hole I was born into and showed readers how I reached what felt like a peak of the Alps. I wrote it zealously to "go and tell," hoping to give God glory by sharing my testimony. The book, however, didn't talk about all the lacerations that re-wounded me and the rocks that crumbled beneath my feet throughout the climb.

I continue writing because I have more good reasons to "tell" than I have reasons not to.

I've been scared to write this book, but I am writing anyway because I want to pursue and tell the truth. We don't heal by falling prey to the manipulations of pharisaical self-righteousness. I do not want to paint my journey as perfect. I will not better my soul and relationship with God, and neither will you, by putting on a fake smile. Veiling the truth only leads to a shallow relationship with God, who wants an ocean-vast and sea-deep relationship with us.

We humans come to full consciousness through shadow-boxing: fighting our invisible or imaginary enemies within us. In this book, I want to make friends with my failings and mistakes and expose my contradictions, some of which still exist today. In this book, I will address lies that have led me to destructive thought and behavior patterns, but I will also show you how they now have less of a hold on me. I say *less* of a hold on me because:

1. Healing is a lifelong process. If we assume we've completely healed, then we stop engaging in the healing process, which prevents us from continual and deeper healing.

2. I, myself, am still healing. And I believe I will be until I am standing eye to eye with my Father in heaven.

This book is about what happens when we break—and how we can find deep healing when we look at the open wounds we *thought* were nearly healed. This book is an act of looking behind the cosmetic and locating the real issues so our foundations do not continue to deteriorate. Together, we will tear down the crumbled walls and rebuild them so the homes we create within ourselves are sturdy and safe places to reside. When we finally find a safe place, we heal; and when we heal, we become safe ourselves.

As you read, you might be asking yourself the same question I'm asking myself: *What makes you, Tori, qualified to talk about healing?* I'm not a psychologist, physiologist, brain surgeon, or therapist. I could brag about my undergraduate psychology minor, but that did not give me the words to write this book. I've written this book because I have been loved back to life.

When I was four, I went into the foster-care system for the first time, but after six months I was reunified with my biological mother. From ages four to twelve, I grew up in a very unpredictable environment that devolved into a dysfunctional and abusive home. I reentered the foster-care system as a teenager and moved through twelve homes until I emancipated the day I turned eighteen, without a family to call my own. Though I eventually met God as my loving Father, and though I was taken in and adopted by my track coach, my younger adult years were engulfed by agonizing mental turmoil; broken relationships; and thoughts of escapism, suicide, and self-hatred. Because I could not simply "take my thoughts captive" and "live, laugh, love" to the fullest, I imagined that I was broken—or worse, that my faith was broken.

But throughout the past few years, I have realized that I am not some kind of atomic bomb filled with the potential to harm myself and those around me. I am not helplessly and hopelessly broken. I am just a human who has loved, has been loved, and has hoped for love. And love, in all its various currencies, hurts. Hurt is not something to be ashamed of or uncomfortable with. Jesus is comfortable with those of us who seem to be unable to escape our pain. He simply wants us to remember how to love; and he wants us to remember that we are easy to love. You are easy to love.

Each chapter of this book will address one of the lies, misconceptions, or misunderstandings that fed the patterns that have left me broken. They have possibly broken you too. In many of these lies I address, I can recognize some bits of truth—but what I've learned about myself is that I'm a little radical. I take things to the extreme, and if you're like me, you need to see these misconceptions completely reframed. Though these stories are mine, they are also yours. I hope they will hold up a mirror so you can see yourself for who and what you truly are—loved.

Recently a young woman that I mentor asked me, "How do you feel God's love?" She paused with tears in her eyes. "I just feel like I've never felt it, but everyone else around me has."

I understand the sentiment and her pain all too well. When I accepted Christ into my heart and dedicated my life to living for him, I expected to feel God's relentless and enduring love instantly, but I didn't . . . for years, actually. But during those years, even when I did not *feel* God's love for me, I believed the truth: He did indeed love me. I would see tiny glimmers of Love in my life, and I would hold on to each glimmer of Love until the next one came along. Then, at some point, the glimmers grew into a bright light that led me to clearly see and feel God's love for me.

I say this because when Jacob and I were restoring our hundred-year-old home, we had all the tools we needed. Jacob taught himself, at a much younger age, how to use those tools, but he had to teach me right then and there. It took me some time to learn how to use the tools well, and it didn't always come as naturally for me as it did for him. Likewise, you might need some time to learn how to use the tools in this book. Be gentle with yourself as you get the hang of it. In time, it will get easier, and restoration will be felt.

I have been restored—not in a miraculous instant, but in a way similar to how we restored our home. Slowly, painstakingly, and tearfully. I have been loved so radically after being so broken that I have healed bit by bit.

It is important to me that you do not envision me standing in a pulpit and telling you how to heal. Instead, I want to sit across from you, holding your hands, and bring you along for the journey. After all, we do not become more loving by learning about love. We become more loving by being loved. These words are my attempt to love you so we might heal together, and I want us to heal so we have a greater capacity to love.

If you see yourself as small or insignificant, if you see your pain as irreversible, or if you are just so aware of your brokenness that you feel powerless even in the presence of God, now is the time to cast yourself on God's love. It is in being wounded that we realize we were never as healed as we thought we were, which puts us right where we belong—in the loving arms of our Abba Father. He gently helps us see the patterns we fall back into time and time again. In our pride, and in our fall, we can gaze up and praise God for not putting us on a throne. He does something much sweeter. He welcomes us into his own safe house. He is calling us home.

SELF-LOVE IS SELFISH

THE REALITY OF HOW I VIEWED MYSELF BECAME FIERCELY evident when I woke up in the hospital, not knowing how I got there, at the age of twenty-three. A soft brown hand held mine. When I followed the arm up to its face, I saw Maddie, one of my dearest friends.

I didn't drink during college, so once I became a full-blown adult, I did not know *how* to drink. As a bridesmaid at my first-ever bachelorette party, I took the drinks that were made for me. I knew they contained alcohol, but I suppose I didn't really know what liquor could do to a 115-pound body in 100-degree weather.

"What happened?" I muttered. The lights in the hospital appeared blurry. I tried to move, but the massive needle in my arm felt more like a sword puncturing my elbow each time I shifted.

Maddie continued to hold my hand and spoke in a monotone as she usually did. "You passed out on the boat."

"What?" I genuinely did not remember.

We had begun the bachelorette party at the bride's in-laws' place, gone to a winery, and by the afternoon, we were back at the in-laws' on a boat. The last thing I remembered was scream-singing the song "Truth Hurts" by Lizzo.

"You completely passed out on the boat. Then you started throwing up and passed out again. When you finally did wake up, you started saying terrible things about yourself—like how you should die and not exist and how you're the worst person to have ever lived. Then you passed out again, and we called an ambulance when we couldn't wake you up."

"Are you kidding me?" I said much too loudly. I shot up from the bed, and the IV dug into my arm.

A nurse rushed in. "You're awake!" she exclaimed.

"Is this real? Like, is this serious?" I shouted. Maddie and the nurse both stared at me.

"Am I actually in the hospital because I got *that* drunk?"

"Yes," they said at the same time.

I was in disbelief. It was hilarious as much as it was embarrassing. "Does insurance actually cover this? Does insurance pay for stupidity?"

The nurse and Maddie started to laugh, which then made me laugh, though I'd been very serious when I asked the question. I smacked my face with my palm and winced as the IV, keeping me hydrated, dug deeper into my arm. I squeezed my eyes closed and hoped I was in some kind of dream. The occasional giggle shimmied through my fingers. Then the nurse and Maddie walked me through what my next steps would be.

After the nurse left, I looked at Maddie and asked, "What did you say I was saying—you know, when I woke up?" She explained that I spoke the worst things she'd ever heard anyone say about themselves.

My mom had a way with words—words so harsh they could have killed. Literally. I was probably ten years old when I grabbed a knife and held it to my neck. I told Mom if she didn't stop screaming insults at me, I'd kill myself. She tackled me to the ground, wrestled the knife out of my hand, and said I needed to go to the psychiatric ward. I never would have done such a thing if those words weren't spoken over me. I just wanted the words to be silenced. Nonetheless, I was the crazy one; in Mom's eyes, I was the problem. In turn, I was always trying to figure out what was so wrong with me so I could fix myself and undo the ruin.

The words my mom spoke over me were hidden in my mind for so long; but the alcohol made the humiliating names dance. They wanted to be seen.

This particular journey of looking deeper and inward started in that hospital bed. I pondered the idea of everything I really thought of myself spewing out. I had been in and out of therapy since I was twelve years old. When I was in the foster-care system, therapy was mandated. I'd even done group therapy and continued therapy into college. I already understood how what was spoken over me as a child had crushed me, but on that day in the hospital bed, I realized I did not know how to love myself or like myself. Despite knowing God, I hated myself.

COMING TO KNOW LOVE

I knew Love. Or maybe I should say Love knew me. Though I did not acknowledge him, he met me many times. Even in the worst of places.

One day, when I was in juvie at the age of twelve, I did not hear the guard yell for roll call. Had I heard him, I would have promptly stood up exactly as I was supposed to. I did not want to get written up, because every write-up was sent to the judge determining how much time I would spend in juvie. And I wanted the judge to release me sooner rather than later.

However, when five loud blows sounded, I was sleeping. I had not heard the six-foot-something guard punching the metal door that rumbled my entire cell. Because I did not do what I was supposed to do right when I was supposed to do it, my book and mattress (which more resembled a gymnastics mat) were taken out of my room. All I had left was a toilet, a concrete slab, and a Bible.

There was nothing to do for the hours of confinement other than leaf through and read God's love letter to me. Love met me through those thin, see-through pages. I even thought, *Paul was in jail. I'm in jail. Everything is going to be all right.* I imagine Love laughed at that. When my consequence was over, I took Love's letters to the common area. Along with the other girls, I read the letters as we ate nearly expired cafeteria food prepared for us by the adult prisoners in the correctional facility next door. In my orange jumpsuit and plastic beige sandals, I told people about the love of God.

Though Love was there all along, I would not see Love for who he was until a decade after he first showed himself. At the age of seventeen, I heard him cry, *Daughter!* His arms were open. Finally, I fell head over heels for his compassionate, caring, and never-ending love.

I did not come to accept Christ in the way many others do. While I'd heard the message that I was sinful and in need of a Savior, I found that truth very hard to accept. I'd heard I was a bad kid for so long while I'd been in foster care. I hoped for someone who would see something good in me. Love knew that, so he stirred my heart when I heard him say through sermons, Scripture, devotions, and songs that he loved me, that he was my Father, and that I was worthy enough to be his daughter. After all, I had been searching for a daddy. When I opened myself up to Love, he did not enter my heart as a man who wanted to fix or judge me while banging his gavel. Through biannual court hearings, probation, and foster care, I'd met men like that, and Love was not them. Love was intimate yet protective, and he was always there, choosing me.

FAKING LOVE

In college, a teammate of mine asked me to have a one-on-one lunch with her, hoping to talk about some problems she was facing with relationships. As she talked, I listened, and occasionally felt my phone vibrate. Despite being in mid-conversation, I picked up my phone and read that another friend needed help moving from her dorm to her sorority house. I genuinely loved being the person others reached out to for help. Though it sounds like a brag on myself, I do believe they knew I would show up. I wanted to help. I wanted to be love in action, so I texted back to let the friend know I would be there to help after lunch.

The friend I was eating with gently confronted me, letting me know she often felt that when I was with her, I was also somewhere else at the same time. She wasn't wrong, and though I don't fully remember what the rest of that lunch looked like, I wouldn't be surprised if I rushed my friend through the rest of her story about what she was going through. I probably offered her quick-fix advice like a Band-Aid, then ran off to the next place I could play hero.

Between classes and track practice, I surrounded myself with people. When I was alone, I felt scared and anxious. Not having a boyfriend magnified my anxiety. I felt like I needed someone to love and needed someone to love me. I'd rationalize dysfunctional relationships and friendships, the unhealthy and unholy dynamics within them, then say it was all for the sake of love. I labeled all my romantic relationships as "true love." I labeled all my close friends as "best friends." Over and over again.

Despite all my good intentions, I look back now and know I used "love"—which really was not Love at all—to cover up the hate I felt for myself. If I was loving and serving others, could I fool myself into believing I wasn't the bad person I truly believed myself to be? In reality, I was actually avoiding being alone and sitting in the quiet with my thoughts. I filled my time serving others to numb the seething pain of my own self-hatred. I was running away from my pain, hurrying through good deeds, because acknowledging my pain, I feared, meant admitting that maybe the God I loved so much—the God who loved me so much—was not real. After all, in church I was learning that God eradicated our pain through his love. The way I understood it, if I was still in pain, I was not loved. I knew the truth was that God loved me, even if I didn't understand his love—so the only reasonable way to reconcile my pain with my faith was to ignore my pain altogether.

HOW HOLY LONELINESS LEADS US TO LOVE

To avoid being alone, I used to beg people to include me. In my loneliness, I'd curl up in my bed and wait for a phone call or text message to be invited. To me, being included meant being loved. Being invited meant belonging. If I couldn't physically be with people, I'd call or text someone to fill the void. I even scheduled my days around being with people.

But after college, my work forced me to spend a lot of time alone. I started to write alone. I started to go on long drives or plane rides by myself for speaking engagements. And I started to go out to eat by myself. I didn't have much of a choice about these situations, but before long I experienced a peace I hadn't before. I'm not sure if I would have ever been brave enough to choose being alone, but I see now how God was designing parts of my work and life to lead me into a holy kind of loneliness. Some spiritual people might call it "solitude," and as uncomfortable as the thought of solitude can be, it became a kind of comfort to me.

Being alone helped me to hear God's kind voice a bit more clearly. In sitting with myself, I've experienced God sitting with me; and by sitting with him, I have learned how to listen to him. I used to sit across from others craving words of acceptance from them. Now I can sit alone, with fewer distractions than I would experience with someone by me, and my mind becomes unbusy and uncluttered enough to hear God. As I have practiced having dates with God while I eat my meals and go on walks, I have come to understand that he doesn't despise me in the ways I despised myself. He actually accepts me, and now I can sit with myself and know the acceptance I have in my Father. No other voices or chatter can make his voice distant. By being alone, I've learned to love who God created me to be.

As I began choosing to love who God created me to be, I noticed I could now show up fully wherever he called. We gain permission to show up fully when we're not attempting to be enough for everyone. The same thing happens when we're not trying to run away from the disdain we have for ourselves or trying to prove ourselves worthy.

So I realized the truth—that I could indeed love who God created me to be—but the thought pattern I kept tripping on was that loving anything about myself would be considered ungodly. As I understood it, I needed to let God take the reins by ridding myself of all I used to be. But the reality is, God made me. He has held the reins from the very beginning, and when he made us, he didn't hate his creation. He even said we are good.[1] To love who God has created us to be is to affirm what God has already said.

> To love who God has created us to be is to affirm what God has already said.

GOD DID A GOOD JOB MAKING YOU

In Mark 12 of the New Testament, a debate was taking place about what is most important in life. Unsure of the right answer, one teacher of the law turned to Jesus and asked: "Of all the commandments, which is the most important?"

"The most important one," Jesus said, is to "'Love the Lord your God with all your heart and with all your soul and with all your mind and with all your strength.' The second is this: 'Love your neighbor as yourself.' There is no commandment greater than these."[2] See, when Jesus points us toward loving our neighbor, it is assumed that we love ourselves. Not in a haughty way, but in a way that makes us able to love God's people as he loves them. Loving who God has created me to be has helped me be more present for those in front of me, rather than be motivated by the need to gain the love I didn't have for myself. God insists that we love ourselves as he loves us and others. That's why I say that self-love, as God loves us, is godly.

Before I understood that I could actually like and love who God created me to be, I was so absorbed with my shortcomings, my mistakes, and how others liked, loved, or perceived me. I was in constant anxiety and fear. But when I gave myself permission to love myself, I felt free from the demeaning voices in my head, the opinions of others, and even my internal self-critic. This is because when your self-critic's lies are silenced, you will begin to hear God's truth.

Proverbs 19:8 says, "To acquire wisdom is to love yourself; people who cherish understanding will prosper" (NLT). You will acquire wisdom when you love yourself, because you will hear the good that God says about you. Rather than being consumed by negative thoughts or what others say, you become more aware of God's truth. When we love ourselves as God loves us, our thought patterns shift from worry to wisdom. God's opinion of you trumps every other opinion—even your own—and his love for you gives you permission to love yourself.

In one hand, I held the truth: "I am truly loved." In the other hand, I held the lie: "To love myself at all would be selfish." I didn't find myself deserving of love because I didn't see myself as good. I thought, *To like myself is to be conceited. To see myself as good is prideful.* But these are lies. God did a good job making me. God did a good job making you. In his love, we are good creations.[3]

God did a
good job
making you.

I have a new mantra for when my thought pattern begins to spiral into self-deprecation, and I want to hand it off to you: "God did a good job making me." When my reflex is to tear my being apart, I say to myself, *Tori, God did a good job making you.*

Understanding his love for us becomes a foundation to build upon. Instead of doing *to* be loved, we do *because* we are loved. Instead of doing to prove ourselves, we do because we know we were made well. Rather than living to be loved, we live freely because we know our identity is beloved. If we trust that God loves us, we stop running from him and start sitting alone with him. When we are in his embrace, we can hear his truth. When we know that truth, we eradicate the lies. When the lies become quieter, we know who God says he is and who he says we are.

How do we break the shackles of self-hatred? By accepting that God loves us already, and that he did a good job making us. Self-love is not some selfish or conceited act. It is God's will for his beloved children.

THE TRUTH ABOUT LOVE

I tend to be driven by accomplishments and accolades. My mom valued high achievement and held high standards for me growing up. From the time I could understand what she was saying, I understood she wanted me to go to college. My being an educated and successful woman was of utmost importance to her. Though people have shamed me for my ambition at times, especially as a woman, I can say that I am generally proud of my ambition and thankful for my mom instilling it in me. I ended up needing it to survive.

Of course, that ambition fueled my desire to be on the best of the best bestseller lists. I often reference publishing my first book, *Fostered*, because the entire process had a profound impact on me. As we were preparing for the book to launch, I met with the publishing team every week—and every week, I told them I wanted to be a bestselling author. This encompasses who I am to the core. I dream the biggest possible dreams, and the goals I have cannot be any smaller than the biggest of what has already been accomplished, even if they are wildly unrealistic.

When I went into the foster-care system, some of my friends' parents wouldn't let their kids hang out with me because I was in foster care. Parents and caseworkers labeled me a bad kid. A troubled child. So I did all I could to prove them wrong—getting the best grades possible, graduating nearly a valedictorian, and training to be a star athlete.

My senior year, I became a four-time state champion in track and field, and the parents of my friends began to change their perspective of me. People in my community who once wanted little to nothing to do with me suddenly cared to get to know me and even befriend me. When I graduated from college, foster parents who had kicked me out came back into my life. When I became more well-known in my career, people wanted proximity to me, and those who had once left came back to apologize and make amends.

Achievements had a way of teaching me that I could bring

people back into my life and make people love me if I earned a great enough accolade.

The night before my first book was set to release, I was ecstatic. Celebrations and parties were planned, and the book already had thousands of preorders. I woke up the next morning, hopped out of bed to grab my phone, and looked for some updates about the book's sales numbers. But to my surprise, the book was not available to purchase anywhere because the book was not in stock.

After frantically emailing my agent, I learned not enough books had been printed to send out to those who'd ordered them—let alone enough to make any bestseller list I was aiming for. People had preordered *that* many more books than what was predicted. And while this sounds great, the result was actually devastating. Retailers were canceling orders they could not fulfill, and now the book could not be ordered at all.

That book was a piece of my heart and soul that I hoped would reach and help people. I'd devoted myself to being a good steward of my launch, but the results were completely out of my control.

Heavy tears rolled down my face until my cheeks glistened and my eyes were red. I knew the book would get into the hands of whomever God intended. I knew God was not concerned with bestseller lists as much as he was concerned with me trusting him, but I couldn't shake the sadness I felt.

So I asked myself, *Why am I so upset?*

With used tissue filling my lap, the tears wouldn't stop. And as I sat in my pain, pondered, and attempted to pray, I realized something: I'd hoped the success of the book might bring people back and earn people's love, as success had always done for me.

During my book launch, there were people I intentionally excluded from my life for about a year because of how unhealthy the relationships had become—but still I missed them and loved them. And deep down, I hoped the book would perform so well that it would compel them to show up, apologize, and make amends.

Accomplishments had become a lifeline of sorts, until I realized accomplishments can't remedy all. The people did not come back, and it wasn't because the book didn't succeed. Eventually it did. The people did not come back because they didn't want to, and because it was not what was best or healthy. It was not rejection of man. It was God's divine protection of me and my family.

The book not hitting the bestseller list I wanted was ultimately good for me. It prompted me to grieve—initially over the launch of my book but also over the relationships I had avoided grieving. The book launch made me face my ambition again, how I'd let it trick me into thinking I could accumulate something greater than God being pleased with my faithfulness. I believed I could earn love, but without my accolade, I realized that no amount of dedication, discipline, drive, or success will earn love—because love is freely given.

Ambition is a powerful force. It dares us to dream, innovate, and do what has never been done. Without ambition, we could live without an aim toward good or beauty, unable to fulfill the purposes God has for our lives. But the two-edged sword of ambition can corrupt us into believing our significance, worth, security, love, and even relationships are rooted in accomplishment rather than our identity in Christ.

The day my book didn't launch how I thought it would, I had to remember again that Jesus died on the cross for everyone—including people who will never accomplish anything. He loves us despite our accomplishments, not because of our accomplishments. The love he has to offer can never be earned. It is accessible to all because it is freely given.

But here's the thing. I knew God loved me. I really did. I'd just never learned how to rest in his love. I could remember it, but I had to learn how to believe it, and that came with continual belief. When my heart didn't believe it, my mind just had to keep convincing me. I learned that we convince ourselves of God's love by telling ourselves the truth. We learn to rest in God's love when we become more comfortable with the truth. And we become more comfortable with the truth the longer we say it over ourselves: *God did a good job making me, I'm mightily loved, and I have permission to love the person he has created me to be.*

LOVE LIKE YOU'VE NEVER BEEN HURT

MY CAR WAS IN PARK, AND MY FOREHEAD WAS PRESSED against the top of the steering wheel. I screamed. No phrases or words poured from my tongue. Just screams. Another relationship in shambles.

As I used all my might to push the pain out through howls, tears flowed down my face. My two children began to cry in the back seat. "Mommy, that scares me," my son mustered. I reached back and laid my hand on his leg. "I'm so sorry, bud. I'm sorry. I didn't mean to scare you." I had to gather myself for the sake of how my children would remember me on this day.

I pressed my foot on the brake, put the car in Drive, and drove forward until I found a long road. I drove slowly in an attempt to regulate myself. The car has been a kind of safe place for me, somewhere I can control the sensory—the temperature, the sounds, the views. Once my littles fell asleep in the back seat, I pulled into the driveway of a warehouse. The tears were falling slower now. I understood why the actions of my friend hurt me, but I was confused about *how* I was hurting so deeply again. After so many times experiencing hurt, I'd hoped I would learn how to avoid it or at least become more immune to it. Yet this time the hurt felt greater than it probably should have.

After a large exhale, I picked up my hefty Bible from the passenger seat. It goes about everywhere with me. The binding is broken, so I am more careful as I leaf through the pages in the back. Its brokenness may be the only characteristic this Bible and I have in common. I've tried to get a new one, but the kind of Bible I have isn't made anymore. The commentary and alphabetical index help me understand more of what I am reading, so I keep it.

I looked up the word *broken*. I flipped through the index, and it guided me to look up Psalm 51:17, which reads, "My sacrifice, O God, is a broken spirit; a broken and contrite heart you, God, will not despise."

I inhale: "God will not despise . . ."; I exhale: ". . . my broken heart." God does not despise our broken hearts.

I like definitions and look them up often. I want to know the meanings, synonyms, and antonyms of words. I also want to know the context. I looked up the word *despise* in an online dictionary and found that some antonyms to the word include *revere* and *like*.[1] I paused to take in this newfound reality. God does not just tolerate our broken hearts. God honors, favors, and likes our broken hearts.

The thin pages of my Bible fell in between my fingers as the alphabetical index showed me the word *brokenhearted* and directed me to Psalm 34:18. It read, "The LORD is close to the brokenhearted."

I inhale: "The Lord . . ."; I exhale: ". . . is close to me." God does not turn away from our brokenness and hurt. He leans in. He honors a broken heart, so maybe I should honor my own.

My hurt, my brokenness, my baggage have all been used against me. People have pointed to my brokenness as the cause of many of the issues I have had. But on this day of brokenness, I realized that our brokenness does not always point to a deficit in us. Sometimes our brokenness points to the disciples we are. Then I asked myself what it might look like for my hurt and brokenness to be honored as God would honor it.

HOW HURTING TRANSFORMS TO HELPING

I spent some years as a child living in a trailer park that others in town saw as a disgraced place.

As an adult, I was attending a weekly prayer gathering at my church one afternoon. While we were in prayer, my pastor pleaded for God to help us know what to do with the trailer park and their "devastating" situation. When the prayer meeting was over, I asked him what he meant. What

> Our brokenness does not always point to a deficit in us. Sometimes our brokenness points to the disciples we are.

was happening at the trailer park? He said, "The trailer park does not have running water. The city has turned it off because the water they are using is contaminated and contaminating other parts of the town. The plumbing has been neglected for so long."

My body started to shake in a way I could feel though no one else could see it.

"What is being done about it? How long do they have to go without water?"

No one in the prayer meeting seemed to have answers.

My heart was heavy and pounding. I hopped on social media to see if I could find any updates on the matter. Sadly, I only found a few comments degrading the management, owners, and residents of the park. Those comments felt like a great injustice and made me feel even more deeply that something must be done. I called the mayor's office while scrolling through Facebook, trying to find any news about the residents' living situations. What typically happens in developing countries was happening right across town. And all I could find online were mean comments from various locals using terms like *trailer trash* and other derogatory names no human should be called. I couldn't help but wonder how little girl Tori would be feeling in that moment—made fun of for living where she did, with her water turned off, unable to take a shower or go to the restroom. No child had any control over this situation or could change it on their own.

The mayor's administration was kind, thanked me for wanting to help, and gave me the trailer park manager's phone number. When I called the manager, Haley, she was instantly and understandably defensive about the plumbing situation, saying she would get it fixed. It was apparent to me that she thought I was another person judging her management and circumstances, rather than someone who could see myself in her shoes and wanted to help.

"I'm so sorry. I can't imagine how much you are carrying." As I sat on the phone with her, I attempted to use as many comforting words as possible. "If you need anything, we really want to help. This has to be such a hard situation." Trying to end the call, she thanked me quickly, in a hurry to remedy her situation and go back to serving those living in her trailer park. I knew before she hung up the phone that I had to be honest with her; if she was going to let me help her, she first had to hear how alike we were.

So I stopped her before she hung up. "Hey. Before we get off the phone, I just wanted you to know I lived in the trailer park when I was a kid." Even over the phone, I could hear her wall crumble and fall.

Her tone softened. "Oh, really?" Finally, she opened up about tangible ways we could serve the community living in the park.

After our call, we texted back and forth to schedule a time for us to bring the residents cases of bottled water and disposable drinking cups. We then went from door to door simply dropping off the supplies.

A man named Eddie stopped us and said, "Hey, I remember you." He pointed to the brown and white abandoned trailer I used to live in with my mom. He spoke my mom's name and said, "I used to mow your lawn."

I smiled and said, "Yes, I remember." We bantered like we were lifelong neighbors.

The next day, Haley posted on Facebook urging the community to stop judging and speaking poorly about those who lived in the trailer park. It was a long post about how people were being affected by harsh words though they were only trying to survive and take care of themselves amid harsh enough circumstances. At the end she wrote, "I want to mention Tori Hope Petersen for reaching out and showing actual concern and empathy. What a wonderful lady. One that knows the difference between saying you care and actually caring. Her help and offering has been a welcome contrast to what we usually receive . . ."

My eyes welled as I read those words. Genuinely, I did care. Deeply. I had lived where they lived, eaten where they ate, slept where they slept, and heard the same degrading comments growing up. And it was far from easy. For me, living in that trailer park was a nightmare—the place where I was abused and my hurt festered. But in this moment, the hurt I'd endured turned into empathy, action, and care for my neighbors. The hurt I had been through allowed me to understand others' hurt. This is proof that our hurt does not have to be a hindrance. With a little healing, our hurt can transform into genuine help.

EMBRACE YOUR BROKENNESS

When we look at the life of Christ, we see that he hurt, too, and he did not hide his brokenness. He showed people his scars. He broke bread to remind us of his breaking, because it was his hurt and brokenness that would direct us back to intimacy with him. He wanted us to remember the hurt.

When Jesus wanted to feed five thousand people, he started with five loaves of bread. When the disciples looked at the five loaves of bread and two fish, they questioned how they would feed all those who hungered, but Jesus *broke* the bread, handed it to his disciples, and miraculously they had enough for everyone.

I imagine us, the most broken, in Jesus' hands. Like the bread being broken, we don't have to go to waste, nor do we come up short. In the hands of our Father, we become more than enough. Our brokenness can be used to feed and replenish the brokenhearted who stand before us too. It's important to remember that God does not like to break us. We break because of the world we live in and the choices we make. But when we put our broken pieces in the hands of Jesus, we can be given to people in a thousand pieces, a thousand different miraculous ways. In our brokenness and hurt, our love is not minimized. It actually has the power to be multiplied into empathy, understanding, and kindness.

Second Corinthians 12:9–10 says, "'My power is made perfect in weakness.' Therefore I will boast all the more gladly about my weaknesses, so that Christ's power may rest on me. That is why, for Christ's sake, I delight in weaknesses, in insults, in hardships, in persecutions, in difficulties. For when I am weak, then I am strong" (ESV). We can even boast in our weakness, and in our hurt, because of what Christ can do with it through his power.

Jesus *broke* bread again as the final Passover supper was ending. He gave it to his apostles, saying, "Take and eat."[2] Then, "This is my body, which is given for you. Do this in remembrance of me."[3] When we break bread, we remember that he broke. To embrace our brokenness is to remember that Christ broke for us. To hurt is to remember Christ hurt for us. May we rest assured that our hurt shall not be wasted, because the greatest act of love was paired with the greatest act of hurt—not hidden but displayed. Our hurt may be our greatest advantage in learning to love.

Christ himself showed us what it would look like for our hurt to be seen and used. Christ loved like he had been hurt. My hope is that we do too.

LOVE LIKE YOU HAVE BEEN HURT

For so long, I thought I needed to just stop hurting. I needed to stop feeling so broken. If I could stop feeling such deep pain in my heart and mind, that would signal that I was healed. The pressure to rid myself of hurt to prove that I was healed would leave me so disappointed anytime I felt angry, sad, or heartbroken. I'd think to myself, *I'm never going to be healed.*

Anytime my hurt peeked through the smallest hole, I'd feel weak and hopeless about the "progress" and "growth" I was supposed to be experiencing throughout my healing journey.

But life has shown me that feeling such deep pain is what moves me to remember to serve the people Jesus loves. My hurt has enabled me to not be like those who write mean slurs on social media about people who are hurting. When we remember our hurt, we want to minimize others' hurt—not add to it.

You've heard the often-repeated adage: "Love like you've never been hurt." While I appreciate the sentiment of these words, I actually think we should love like we have been hurt. Because in doing so, we acknowledge our own hurt. We have to face our pain. Because in doing so, we gain awareness of how not to hurt others in the same ways. Then our hurt, transformed to love, becomes a gift to us and those around us.

In the trailer park, it was common knowledge that the people running the place had put others' livelihoods at risk due to the contaminated water. It wasn't right or fair, but my hurt is what urged me to not inflict more pain onto an already painful situation. While others may focus on how "bad" people are, our past experiences of pain remind us of how human we all are. When we fully acknowledge our wounds, our hurt does not control us through triggers; rather, our hurt motivates us to serve those who have been through what we have.

It is possible to see our hurt not as heavy baggage to be dragged behind us or hidden in a closet, but as something to be dug through and observed. In this way, we gain power over each pain point, piece by piece. We better understand ourselves and the people around us, and we can love them deeper. The garbage that people shamed us for begins to glisten because it was never garbage at all. What naysayers may have put us down for can be the very thing we use to lift others up.

Our hurt, when honored and not hidden, may be our greatest asset to our relationships. Brokenness can lead to empathy and understanding. Our own hurt grants us the right amount of anger that forces our bodies to shake uncontrollably, call city officials, and do something. Plus, showing others our hurt makes them more willing to show us theirs. Our own hurt transformed has the power to heal someone else. Our hurt—in all its honor and glory—can be the vigor behind every act of love we give.

This is what it means to love like we have been hurt: to love like Christ crucified. God made himself man so he would *know* our pain—not just in a way of being all-knowing, but in a way of bearing it himself. Because Christ first loved us through the agonizing pain of the cross, love is what we can become after failings, fallings, humility, lessons, holding on, and even being hurt.

A PRAYER FOR THE BROKEN ONE

May your victimhood make you a victor.

May your poverty inspire you to care for the impoverished.

May the battles you've endured forge you to be a warrior.

May the curses spoken against you be the fuel that burns generational curses.

May orphanhood compel you to be a worshipful child of God.

May earthly fatherlessness teach you to readily depend on your Father in heaven.

May your own broken pieces mend others' broken hearts.

May the times you have felt unloved cause you to never cease loving.

TO LOVE IS TO BE VULNERABLE, ALWAYS

AFTER MY FRESHMAN YEAR OF COLLEGE, I WORKED IN a diner waiting tables. Though I had been drawn toward God through people and church and the Bible in my jail cell, and though I could see him pursuing me throughout my life, my salvation and relationship with Jesus did not begin until I was seventeen, about a year and a half prior to this job. I had been consistently going to church. I wanted to actively live like Jesus, and I felt like waiting tables was the perfect opportunity for me to shine the light of Jesus onto people who may not know him. I did my work joyfully, with 1 Corinthians 10:31 in mind: "Whatever you do, do everything for the glory of God" (csb).

Wearing my large cross necklace, and with a smile on my face, I served everyone to the best of my ability. Though I didn't get to know the people I waited on well, I hoped the kindness I showed, and the way I served, left a mark. I hoped it would make them wonder about what I had in my heart. And I hoped they would remember the cross necklace I wore around my neck and think of Jesus.

I worked swing shifts, so I got to know most people I worked with relatively well, especially the other waitresses. My intention with them was the same as it was with my customers: to love them well so they would know Jesus loves them. To do so, I'd imagine a piece of paper stuck to the person's forehead that read, "Please make me feel important." People *are* important, so I wanted to make them feel that way!

One afternoon after the lunch rush was settled, around two thirty, another waitress around my age sat down with me to eat our late lunch. Between bites of burgers and wiping grease from my lips, I asked Shelly about her life, if she was in school, if she wanted to keep waitressing, and so on.

She told me she actually had another job bringing in good money, and she wanted to continue doing it. Wanting to show interest in her life and passions, I asked her what she did.

"Well, do you have plans tonight?" she asked me.

I said, "No! Why?"

She smiled a wide, inviting smile, and her eyes lit up. "You should come and watch me. I dance!"

To avoid any awkward silence, and not wanting her to feel judged, I quickly said, "Of course! I'd love to!"

When she said she was a dancer, I knew exactly what she meant. Later that afternoon, I thought up all sorts of ways I could bail. I knew stripping wasn't something I should support, but I didn't even have her number to text her the lame lie that I was sick. As time went on, I had to decide whether I should ghost her but then face her at work, or go and prove to her that I wasn't afraid to show up for her. I thought if my intention was to let her know she was loved and important, I had to show my love by showing up.

When I arrived, I winced as I placed a twenty-dollar bill in the bouncer's large hand. My hard-earned tips were enriching a corrupt business that exploited women, and it made my stomach sink. I was aware that money has power, and people make a difference by spending their money with purpose. At one point in college, I'd even tried to boycott fast-fashion brands—but here I was spending my money in a strip club. My hands began to shake as I walked through the dark room. The smells nauseated me, giving me instant, millisecond flashbacks to the motel that Mom left me in as a little girl.

My intention was to wave at my coworker, show my "support," and say goodbye. The place was flooded with people. From the moment I entered the door and walked from the entrance to the stage, men approached me. One put his hands around my waist without asking. I smiled and pushed him off. Another smacked my butt and grinned when I shot him a grimace.

I continued to walk forward, wondering why getting to Shelly was taking so long. I was holding on to the belief that my love would be enough for this woman to change her lifestyle and follow Jesus. Smiling and waving at Shelly, I approached the stage, chatted, and gave her a hug as she wore nearly nothing. After she started dancing, I left, hoping she wouldn't notice my absence.

That night I struggled to sleep. The experience brought back traumatic memories from my childhood in ways I could not have anticipated. Even though I tried to push the flashbacks out, the images kept replaying in my mind throughout the days to come. I couldn't shut them off. Thankfully, they eventually faded away in their own time.

Had I been self-aware enough to know that my trauma would be triggered in this situation, or had I seen my hurt for what it was, I also would have seen how similar the situations I had been in were to Shelly's. I would have understood that Shelly was being hurt, and my hurt would have turned into the superpower of being brave enough to ask her if she needed a way out. I could have taken action to protect both of us. But instead, I shoved my pain down, put on a smile, and hoped that playing hero would save the day. I believed my love would change her rather than believing God's love would do the job.

Some people are equipped and called to step into these spaces and minister to women stuck in this lifestyle. However, I know now that I was hopeful to play hero because I not only walked into harmful situations like this one with Shelly, but I also repeatedly entered dysfunctional relationships while believing I could save the hurting person.

This kind of "love" damages us. It points others to ourselves rather than pointing people to Christ. In fact, it draws us further from the heart of God, endorsing what is harmful rather than calling the harm what it is. It often exposes and exploits rather than protecting and taking care. Loving this way puts us in dangerous positions, but as God's children, we are worth protecting.

Luke 11:34 says, "Your eye is the lamp of your body. When your eye is healthy, your whole body is full of light, but when it is bad, your body is full of darkness" (esv). That night in the strip club, what I saw with my eyes was dark and sad. I felt full of darkness for weeks to come. What I exposed myself to triggered a flood of uncontrollable memories. With my eyes, I let the darkness in.

Now, in hindsight, I'm sure I could list the many ways I could have done better. Couldn't we all? But my point here is not to berate myself or anyone else who has gone into places they shouldn't have, or to shame women who have worked in those spaces. My point is that our hearts are fragile—and sometimes, in love, we must kindly and truthfully protect ourselves. And in doing so, we can protect others too. In humility, we can confess that we cannot handle it all and we're not meant to save others.

I don't want you to hear this from me as you might have heard it before, screamed through microphones and megaphones or placed on condemning billboards and picket signs. I say these words with a sigh, hoping you will feel the utter relief that you do not have to carry the burden: *Only God can save.*

I know now that Shelly and I are not so different after all. My past gave me a blueprint for how to love Shelly and point her to the truth, but I missed it because I misunderstood what vulnerability meant.

Looking back now, I wish I would have asked Shelly questions like "What draws you toward that job?" Or "What are you hoping to get out of the work?" These questions would have helped me understand her heart and then guide her toward what she truly wanted out of life. If I could rewrite that conversation, I'd say, "I understand you so much more now, but I don't think that is a safe place for me. I also do not think it is a safe place for you. Even though I can't come to the strip club, I want to be here for you in other ways."

Maybe some people will think this is too direct. But does love allow a neighbor to be exploited? Does love endorse God's beloved falling away from him? Does love remain silent to sin—to things that are hurting another person?

While writing this story, I couldn't help but wonder, *Where is Shelly now, and wherever she is, how did she get there?* Through some online searching I found that she had her own family and had given her life to Christ. Eventually, I messaged her and asked, "What turned your life around?"

She replied quickly and boldly, telling me the story of how the lifestyle of being a stripper was dark and dangerous—but mainly because of the financial aspect, she did not know how to get out of it. At one of her lowest points, she called a Christian hotline, and the woman who answered told her directly and clearly to get out of the strip club and work somewhere else. At the time, Shelly was pregnant and couldn't find a job anywhere. It was widely known that she was a stripper.

Regardless, she took the woman's counsel, left the club, and eventually found a job. She knew she wanted a different life for her own family. She started going to church again and re-dedicated her life to Jesus. And it all started with someone telling her the truth.

God gives commandments not to condemn us but to give us protective guidelines like a good Father would. He's not slamming a rule book in our faces, shouting, "Don't walk in there!" He is holding our hearts in his hands, taking the best care of us. God is not a bigot. He is the guardian of his children.

Proverbs 4:20–23 says,

> My son, pay attention to what I say;
> turn your ear to my words.
> Do not let them out of your sight,
> keep them within your heart;
> for they are life to those who find them
> and health to one's whole body.
> Above all else, guard your heart,
> for everything you do flows from it.

Our human hearts can be easily broken when we expose them to any and all situations. If not broken, they are molded into odd shapes by careless hands grazing our waists and slapping our butts without a care for how and who God created us to be. Surely, we must love people, but we cannot override God's love. When we love God most, we will love people as he commands us to.

HOW TO GUARD YOUR HEART

While in foster care, I lived in a group home with nine other girls. The doors were always locked. Authorized people were allowed inside, and others were welcomed only under certain circumstances. Many of the girls had experienced extreme abuse, and some had been victims of trafficking. These rules were set in place to protect all of us who lived in the home.

Our hearts mirror the same kind of home. Imagine a home that holds and shelters God's beloved children. The doors would be open during limited hours. Certain people would have keys to the building, and only people who are safe for the children would be allowed inside. The doors would not be open 24-7 to whomever, whenever, without protection.

Think of our hearts as houses for ourselves, God's beloved children. When we open the doors, giving anyone and everyone access to the building, we easily bring damage upon ourselves. The house can become so damaged that it can no longer protect us. This is why, like houses, our hearts need a guard. The guard comes from living close to God and building our lives on him. This doesn't mean we are not open to others. This doesn't mean we don't share our hearts with people. But it does mean humbly admitting that we are limited human beings whose hearts are not meant to be exposed to all.

I've asked so many times, "How do we guard our hearts without locking our hearts away? How do we protect ourselves while loving vulnerably as we are meant to as Christians?" In Scripture we can often find instruction in the context surrounding the command. Let's revisit the place where we are instructed to guard our hearts, where the Bible tells us

> My son, pay attention to what I say;
>> turn your ear to my words.
> Do not let them out of your sight,
>> keep them within your heart.[1]

We guard our hearts by turning our eyes and ears toward God's Word. We will discern when to guard our hearts and when to be vulnerable the more our senses are turned toward God. Paying attention to the Holy Spirit and keeping his Word in sight will guide and guard us.

The acclaimed Christian author C. S. Lewis wrote, "To love at all is to be vulnerable."[2] This is a quote I clung to, using it to excuse how I overexposed myself to people and places that took my ears and eyes away from God. I rationalized my actions by claiming that I was being vulnerable rather than irresponsible.

Part of this confusion stems from how the idea of *vulnerability* has shifted in our modern culture. The word *vulnerable* is derived from the Latin noun *vulnus*, which means "wound." *Vulnerable* means "capable of being wounded."[3] But the idea of vulnerability has evolved in its usage. We now discuss vulnerability when referring to one being emotionally or spiritually open with someone else. The word has become synonymous with sharing one's life and experiences, especially emotionally, with a risk of being judged or rejected.

The vulnerability we express by sharing the rawest parts of our stories typically helps us relate and connect to others. When people open their hearts to us, we witness Christlikeness and see God working in the lives of others. Sitting with a friend; sharing the real struggles you face with your mental health, family, or vocation; crying on a friend's shoulder as you grieve a loved one; or letting someone into your home when it is messy—and watching them accept and love you through it all—is the kind of vulnerability that heals us.

But being vulnerable means we can be *wounded*—which happens when we are exposed to abuse, exploitation, and destruction of God's creation. This kind of exposure imprints on our brains, doing damage that requires time and intentional effort to repair. While the Christian life will undoubtedly include suffering, God does not want his children to be abused and exploited. If you're paying for a woman's booty to be twerkin' and poppin' in your face before men take her backstage, God's Word has left your sight and you have made yourself *dangerously* vulnerable.

When we become so vulnerable that we struggle to see God or draw close to him, God gives us permission to guard our hearts from the places and people affecting us. Our hearts are meant to be more protected than we might think. Just like a father wants to protect his daughter's heart when she starts dating, God wants to protect his children's hearts from corruption and demise.

After so many relationships where I thought I could save the one I wanted to love, I eventually realized I couldn't.

Time and time again, I entered dangerous places and stayed with unsafe people for the sake of being vulnerable. I realize now that love has the wisdom to discern when to be vulnerable and when to guard one's heart. I am not saying we should keep secrets or live closed lives, but we should protect ourselves from certain places and people. Sometimes, to love is to be vulnerable, and other times, to love is to protect.

> Sometimes, to love is to be vulnerable, and other times, to love is to protect.

Love is not putting ourselves in destruction's way, then masking it by labeling it *vulnerability*. Many of us who fall prey to this pattern were not protected when we were children or when we were supposed to be protected. Let me emphasize: You deserved to be protected during the times you weren't. And it's difficult to learn how to guard our hearts and protect ourselves when no one else modeled the practice for us. But in Jesus' name, you have permission to protect yourself now and let God's Word guide you as you discern where and when to guard your heart.

SOMEDAY IS BETTER THAN TODAY

FOR SO LONG, I WAS TRULY A VICTIM, BEATEN BY THE same hands that held me. Curses were spoken over me by the same mouth that swore love for me. Many of us are real victims of real abusers, but many of us also struggle to escape the worst abuse even when given the opportunities and resources to do so.

I want to be so clear in saying that those who abuse us are absolutely responsible for their actions. They should face consequences for what they've done. Still, in my story, while there are perpetrators who caused me unjustifiable pain, I choose to focus on myself because I'm the only person I can control.

Through gentle revelations from God, I came to see that once we are victimized by others, we can fall prey to victimizing ourselves. The truth is, I played a large part in my own self-destruction by not taking responsibility and agency where I could. I often returned to what destroyed me. This is one of the many effects of complex trauma.

My habit of self-destruction was easy to ignore because I was, by the world's standards, pretty successful. When I graduated from college I viewed myself as emotionally aware and healed. I was proud to be a part of the 3 percent of former foster youth to receive a bachelor's degree.[1] As a four-time state champion in high school and an all-American track athlete in college, I perceived my accomplishments as a barometer that measured how healed I was. Sprinting and winning was a way I'd run away from acknowledging the contusions and abrasions still on my heart from my first family, foster care, and fornicating.

I won a lot of medals. And as those medals were placed around my neck, right over my chest, they covered the true condition of my heart. Many of the achievements I sought out, especially in my track career, I hoped would be avenues to bring glory to God. It's true that God can be glorified in our accomplishments—but while I chased my accomplishments, I did not chase God with the same quickness and endurance. I rarely questioned how I was doing internally because, externally, I checked the boxes and then some. Anything that makes us look successful, polished, and triumphant to the world can draw a veil over our wounds and reality.

Some people who grow up in abusive homes close themselves off, but I trusted everyone in hopes of finding someone. The merry-go-round of false hope carried me through the cycle of seeking love and acceptance, then facing rejection a hundred times over. Serial dating deepened my wounds, but it also numbed me very well. It was easy to ignore my deep feelings of loneliness and the harmful ways I tried to fill the voids. These patterns of clinging to relationships eventually led me to meet and date Jacob. He was also a senior at the college I was attending.

Our school regularly allowed chosen students to have lunch with the college president. One afternoon during my senior year, I was chosen for one of those lunches. In general, the students at my college came from affluent backgrounds and had received quality high school educations. They often spoke about history, politics, and philosophies I struggled to wrap my head around. For that reason, I sat in silence for most of the lunch, listening rather than speaking, until the president of the college asked me what I wanted to do after I graduated. To be honest, I felt so nervous about giving him my answer that I thought about lying. But I didn't have time to think of a lie, so I explained to him that I would like to enter a ministry for those underserved in the foster-care system because I had also grown up in foster care. In response, he offered me a round-trip plane ticket to Alabama, where I would visit a ministry that housed children coming from dysfunctional and abusive families.

The ministry was a ranch with a handful of foster homes, where Christian houseparents lived and raised and cared for the kids. The morning of my arrival at the ranch, the house-parents started the day with worship and prayed for the children they served. I was blown away because I couldn't remember a time when I heard foster parents praying for the children in their care more than they complained about them. The presence of God was powerful and palpable. I thought, *I could have used a place like this when I was a kid.* And if I were to guess God's thoughts, I'd say maybe he thought I needed a place like that right then and there.

I visited that day with no expectations or hopes beyond learning from their programs, parents, and leadership. But after I spent the day with the leaders of the organization, they offered me a job. They had very little knowledge of who I was or why I was there, but the meeting and job offer felt God-ordained. Many people came to visit the ranch regularly to understand its gospel-centered model and check out the programs before committing to donorship or even building their own children's home. I was still in my first semester of senior year. With not too much idea of what my next steps would be, I was being offered a dream job before I had even searched for one.

I gratefully and excitedly accepted the job. When I told my adoptive dad, he beamed with pride for me. My extended family celebrated the announcement, and the president of my college was pleased with the result of his generosity.

Then, in the second semester of my senior year, my pattern of promiscuity changed my plans. With a baby in my belly, I was set to marry Jacob a week after college graduation. I made it known to the leadership of the organization that Jacob and I were getting married without telling them we were having a shotgun wedding. I was hoping to keep the position they had offered to me. But unfortunately, they decided I could no longer come work for them. I suspect they knew I was pregnant, but the position also required me to live with the teenage girls as if I was a residential assistant in their dorm. They did not want me to live there with a man, which was understandable.

The job was not glamorous to many, but I held it in my heart believing it was exactly what I was supposed to do. I thought it would bring me healing and bring glory to God in that season. I still believe this job was God's plan for my life, but because of my disobedience, God let me experience the consequences of my sin. When the executive director told me that I no longer could take the position, Jacob and I sat in disbelief; we were frozen. The only parts of our world that seemed to be moving were the hidden baby in my belly and the tears flowing from our eyes.

I don't think I intentionally ruined the opportunity. No part of me wanted that end result. But this much-needed consequence opened my eyes to why I tended to self-destruct. I was prone to focusing on and glorifying the potential in my life rather than appreciating what I was guaranteed in the present. Whenever boyfriends left, I would find myself with no friends because I'd neglected my friendships. I was drawn toward instability and people who did not commit to me because the approval and security I sought through other means—like my faith, family, community, or opportunities— never felt like enough. I obsessed over the potential of what *could* be rather than what *was*. Then what was present would eventually dissipate because I poured all of myself into what could be.

It's been years since I met with the people at this organization. I'm still waiting for a more redemptive story—one where God can show us why I met them and why it all fell apart. Maybe he will put it all back together. But the story still feels unfinished.

But, for the first time in my life, I understood how heartbreaking the consequences of not obeying God could be. I understood that chasing unpromised potential rather than gratefully accepting where God has positioned me has consequences. The sin of seeking people's love more than I sought God's love could put dents in the beautiful gold plates God is so graciously carving my story into. After so many dents, the story God is writing becomes illegible—but never ruined beyond his ability to buff out.

PERHAPS YOU WERE MADE FOR SUCH A TIME AS THIS

Esther was an orphan who was raised by her cousin Mordecai before being chosen to be queen in the Persian capital of Susa. During her reign, it came to her cousin's attention that another ruler planned to kill all the Jewish people. So Mordecai asked Esther to use her power as queen to approach the king and save the Jewish people. When he asked Esther, he added, "If you remain silent at this time, relief and deliverance for the Jews will arise from another place, but you and your father's family will perish. And who knows but that you have come to your royal position for such a time as this?"[2] Mordecai clearly pointed to the fact that God does not need us. We are blessed enough to be aids in carrying out his will, but if we do not find his present plans to be good enough, he will fulfill his good plans and purpose through someone else.

When we look at the story of Esther in Scripture, we see that God indeed does give us a choice to follow his plan for our lives. We can accept the gift of being instruments in his hands and vessels of his love, or we can disobey and say no. (Saying no usually comes through our rebellious actions, not necessarily words.) But in our disobedience, he is not worried, because he does not need us. He can and will choose someone else to carry out his mission.

Esther showed herself faithful by fasting, approaching the king, and advocating for the marginalized people to be saved. Newly married with a newborn, I began to wonder what could have been had I showed myself faithful and grateful for God's plan instead of fearful, seeking man's love and unpromised potential. What could happen if we all lived as if we were made for such a time as this rather than for such a time that may or may not be?

I think the best we can do is start with today and embrace the present. This day matters just as much as the potential place we could someday be. Instead of looking for possibilities, we could open our eyes to the gifts, opportunities, and people we have right in front us. God has a good plan for your life, and it isn't next year or in five years. Your life doesn't begin when you get the dream job or when you accomplish that goal or when you finally get married or have your next child. God's good-enough plan is in today. When we embrace today as good enough—and live as if we were made for this time and not another—we finally become who we were meant to be.

> God's good-enough plan is in today.

To approach the king and request he not kill the Jewish people, Esther had to first receive his permission. The king could have denied her, or worse, he could have punished her. The queen who reigned before Esther was named Vashti, and she had been uncrowned basically because she stood up for herself to the king. Esther ran the same risk. She could have cared more about continuing her reign than God's plan; but instead, she bravely approached the king and saved an entire nation. Esther became who she was meant to be because she embraced what was—not what could have been.

THE KEY TO CONTENTMENT

Today, I am an author, speaker, and Bible teacher. I have the honor of keynoting events to raise funds for suffering and vulnerable people. I also get to share God's Word at conferences and churches.

For the past few years, I have hoped to be invited to one

specific event. It is a Christian women's conference with thousands of attendees, and several of my friends and cohorts attend and speak at it.

One year, on the same weekend of this big, awe-inspiring conference, I was asked to preach at an intimate retreat for about eighty moms struggling through their motherhood journey. I had not been invited to the big conference. While on my way to the small town to speak to a room of eighty women, I thought of the room of eight thousand women in a big city and felt a tinge of discouragement. Thoughts transpired in my mind like

- *You will never belong in the big room.*
- *You're too rough around the edges.*
- *You're not good enough.*
- *You'll never be good enough.*

Every time I looked on social media, I saw a post from one of my many work friends, speaker friends, and preacher friends about having a wonderful time at the big conference. Now, I'm only human. I wasn't unfazed by this. We are all prone to human desires. But in this situation, I had a choice to make. I could be thankful for the opportunity I was given, or I could wish to be somewhere else. I could focus on the bigness of that other place or devote myself to the present—to those dear women. I could fall into my old patterns of believing that what I had wasn't good enough. I could give a subpar talk and go home—but doing so would have not only been a way of self-destructing; I also would have robbed the women who were in front of me of what they showed up to receive. In the past, these voices and the tension I felt would have taken my focus off my assignment. I would have believed the voices, which would have negatively affected the work I was meant to be present for. But I had learned this lesson before, and I wasn't going to let unhealthy patterns rule this day.

If you're the uninvited, if you're rarely included by the cool kids, or if you're craving what could be rather than what is, I want to share with you some truths. I use these words to combat the lies in hopes that they will help me remain present when I question my assignment—and I hope they will do the same for you.

To keep my focus on the assignment before me, I say to myself:

- *It's not that you don't belong there. It's just that you belong right here.*
- *It's not that you aren't good enough to be there. It's simply that God wants you right here, because these are his kids too. For some reason, whether for lack of resources or time, these children of God couldn't make it to the other place. Instead they ended up here, and they need someone to speak into them.*
- *As much as those are God's kids, these are God's kids too. Show up as such.*
- *Environment does not change the value of your work, and neither does it change the value of God's beloved kids.*

"These are God's kids too" is the short mantra I still repeat to myself today for two reasons:

1. I need to be reminded that my work is not about me or accolades. This life is about serving God and his kids faithfully. Many of the people who have had the greatest influence on me live ordinary lives, allowing people into their homes and living as examples of love. They don't have flashy titles or rewards. Their ministry and work may not be applauded by the world, but I know God sees their effort for what it is. Our society is so concerned with titles and numbers, but God is concerned about our hearts.

2. No matter the environment where we are serving— whether it is mundane, extravagant, ordinary, spectacular, big, or small—we are serving God's kids.

These mindsets have given me a gift of contentment in all that I do.

After I taught that evening to that small room in that small town, I prompted women to pray over one another. Weary women worshiped and wept at the altar as they held each other. Vulnerability grew into victory. As I looked at the room from the stage, I knew I was, indeed, right where I belonged. Maybe, just maybe, you are right where you belong, beloved.

Finding contentment is an intentional, internal fight, but contentment makes us more aware of what God is doing in the here and now and less worried about what we *might* have there and then. God may be trying to bring you healing with what you have, right where you are. Like he showed Esther, God may be trying to show you your purpose through the assignment and people he has set right in front of you. The future or the potential plan might seem better, but the present may be the gift God has been trying to give all along.

TIME HEALS ALL WOUNDS

LIKE MOST COUPLES IN THEIR FIRST YEARS TOGETHER, my husband and I were quite poor when we got married, so we took every free opportunity we could. Free food. Free one-week gym memberships. Free furniture off the side of the road. We took it all.

One afternoon, Jacob found a flyer for a free luncheon, so of course we went. As we ate, a man began speaking about trauma. This was relevant in our marriage considering we'd both had our fair share. And despite time passing, we didn't seem to be as healed as we'd hoped to be.

I listened to the speaker intently. Much of what he said I had learned in my psychology classes or knew from my own therapy experience, but still I struggled with regulating my emotions, especially when an incident reminded me of my upbringing.

It had been nearly twelve years since I had lived with my abuser, yet I was still experiencing unwanted ruptured relationships in my life. Twelve years had passed, yet my triggers felt more tender than ever before. I had heard that time healed all wounds, but at the age of twenty-four, when I was supposed to be in my prime of health, time seemed to have only intensified and magnified my emotional wounds. Through countless heartbreaks and letdowns, I had to come to terms with the reality that time does not heal.

Finally, the speaker said something I'd never heard: Those who grow up in abusive homes are more likely to seek out and be in abusive relationships.[1] In addition, those whose parents abused substances are more likely to marry people who abuse substances.[2] At first this statistic made no sense to me; dysfunction was exactly what I said I did *not* want in relationships, especially for my family and children. Yet the speaker was right. At this point in our lives, Jacob was still struggling with alcohol addiction,* and many of the people I was in close relationships with struggled with extreme dysfunction. How had this happened without my even knowing? Then the speaker said what made even more sense: Those who have been abused enter dysfunctional relationships because it is what their brains are used to. Brains that have experienced

---

* I consciously choose not to tell more of this story despite my husband's openness because it feels like his story rather than mine. One of the most powerful avenues to my healing has been telling my story and understanding it through means of others hearing it. It is important to me that I do not take that from him. I believe that in God's perfect timing, this story will come to light and God will be glorified through my husband. For that reason, this story is not mine to tell more than I have at this time.

constant dysfunction in their upbringing often find comfort in dysfunction.

This research also speaks to something broader and deeper than toxic relationships and substance abuse: specifically that we gravitate toward what we are comfortable and familiar with, whether we want to or not. Whether it's healthy for us or not.

I've said it previously, but I want to be sure I am understood: When we are abused by someone, that person is responsible for their actions. However, we are responsible for our healing afterward because personal accountability is a path to freedom. Part of that responsibility and accountability is taking a gentle look at ourselves and asking, *What is my pattern? What might I depend upon to numb my pain, though behind the curtain, my dependence is intensifying my pain?* I had to ask myself, *What might I be drawn to that brings me comfort to the point that I can't even understand how it is hurting me? What have I become so accustomed to that I don't even see its damage?*

In the past I have explained how complex trauma can result in unhealthy patterns. In response, people suggested that the expression of these unhealthy patterns sounds like excuse making or rationalizing poor behavior. Because of these assumptions, it's important I mention that understanding the way our trauma manifests and where it originates doesn't excuse our choices or negative patterns. Rather, understanding our trauma helps us understand ourselves and begin to heal.

At that moment, as I listened to the speaker, I finally understood my patterns. I had approached my relationships like I was invincible. I typically rationalized returning to toxic patterns by believing that I was loving others and refusing to give up on them, when really I was enduring harmful relationships because I found comfort in them. This left me in a mental hole, and I had no tools to dig myself out. But learning why I did what I did was like having a shovel thrown to me at the bottom of the hole. I could slowly dig a ramp back up with the newfound knowledge I had. Understanding our patterns is a tool for healing, and changing our lives starts with changing the patterns within it.

JESUS ADDRESSES OUR PATTERNS TOO

In the book of John, Jesus met the woman at the well. He showed her immense love and intentionality by meeting her where she was. He didn't wait for her to chase him or meet him somewhere along the way. He went directly to her. When he first encountered her, his disciples had gone into town, which allowed Jesus to spend special, undistracted, one-on-one time with the woman. They were bound to bond.

Of course, when the woman and Jesus spoke, Jesus told her about the life-giving water that would make her thirst no more—meaning he told her about himself. He began a relationship with her and told her she didn't have to seek any other water because the water he offered would quench her thirst. From here, they could have celebrated their relationship, her newfound faith in the Living Water, and moved on. Then she could have gone and told everyone of the man she'd met, preaching the gospel and fulfilling her purpose. Instead, Jesus paused and took the conversation in an unexpected direction.

Jesus acknowledged the woman's patterns.

He did so by bringing up the man she lived with and pointing out that he was not her husband. He then revealed that he knew about her five *prior* husbands. Some scholars will suggest that the woman at the well was adulterous, while others will argue she was widowed many times over. However, I don't think it matters so much. Whether her husbands were lost through circumstance or by choices someone made, there was a pattern in this woman's life that Jesus chose to address. Likewise, whether we create the patterns in our life or the patterns happen to us, they can have drastic effects. Jesus addressed the woman's pattern in order to help her find hope apart from it.

Jesus very well could have brought up any other facts he knew about the woman—the day she was born, where she lived, a family member or friend's name—but he chose to point out a pattern in her life. We also know that Jesus used analogies and stories all throughout Scripture to teach his disciples and followers how to live. Here, Jesus used the analogy of water to point the woman away from depending on what is earthly and toward depending on him—the only one able to satisfy her deepest needs.

It seems the woman at the well had some kind of pattern in her life that did not quench her thirst. Whether she pursued relationships that continued to fall short or lost her husbands by other means, I believe she was experiencing unfulfillment due to the patterns. I imagine she didn't just feel unfulfillment either; so many people passing out of her life must have left her pretty brokenhearted. Jesus the healer was showing her that no relationship outside of him could fulfill her. It would leave her thirsty still.

Jesus is also pointing *us* away from depending on man or any other fleeting earthly desire, and instead, he is pointing us toward depending on him, who alone can satisfy us.

Today, it is estimated that women in developing countries walk an average of three and a half miles a day to get water.[3] It is possible that the woman at the well also walked miles to retrieve water. Imagine: She was thirsty, so she went to fetch water, but the walk depleted her even more. Carrying water back even after she drank plenty at the well would, again, make her thirsty. Getting to the well made her need even more. She was in a cycle. She needed the water to survive. And when we become dependent on anything other than God, we can feel we need it to keep going. This is why Jesus pointed to the relationship he knew could fulfill her and keep her. His life-giving water would overflow her cup. Jesus was the one who would suffice.

Jesus' intent with the woman here was the same intent he has with us. He does not pick at us; rather, Jesus comes to us intimately, one-on-one, to let us know that he chooses

us despite our patterns. He chooses to pro-
vide for us and love us in a way nothing else
and no one else can. He wants us to see and
eradicate our own patterns so we may find
fulfillment in an intimate relationship with
him. We find deep healing when we break
out of our earthly dependencies—drugs,
alcohol, work, other people, and beyond—
and instead commit ourselves to believing
God is enough to depend upon.

> Jesus comes to us intimately, one-on-one, to let us know that he chooses us despite our patterns.

A DEEP DEPENDENCY

When I was sixteen, I convinced my mom to take me to get
my belly button pierced. The piercer took a brand-new, clean,
hollow needle out of the package and shoved it right through
my navel. Then he handed me aftercare instructions, which
said to wash the wound with purified water. But it felt like too
much trouble to go to the store and purchase purified water,
so I used the easily accessible bottle of rubbing alcohol and
rinsed my belly button with it regularly. (I learned this from
Mom, who would douse any wounds I had in rubbing alcohol.
It stung a little, but I never thought it hurt that bad.) Despite
the disinfectant qualities of rubbing alcohol, my belly button
kept getting more and more red. Then, after just a few days,
it grew swollen with puss and hurt so bad that the next best
option was to remove the piercing.

I could have left it in with the hope and belief that the piercing would heal in time, but I know now that without proper care, the infection only would have spread.

Determined to be among the "cool girls" who had their belly buttons pierced in high school, I went back six or so months after the wound healed. The needle had to be thrust through scar tissue on the second go-round, which made me wince much harder than the first time. I most definitely did not want to face the piercer yet again, so I used purified water to clean the wound this time. With that, the piercing healed quickly.

The wound healed because purified water has the power to heal. Something not noted explicitly in the story of the woman at the well is that clean water not only quenches thirst but also has the power to heal. When pure water is poured over open wounds, it washes out infection. Jesus' pure water has the same qualities. He heals us, washing out what separates us from him.

When Jesus pointed out the woman's patterns and showed her how much he knew about her, it made her believe in him all the more. It made her want his Living Water, and she wanted to tell others about it. In her testimony, she basically said, "I know he was legit because he knew me."[4] This interaction spurred her on to boldly tell people about Jesus, and she became the first woman to evangelize in John's Gospel.

I hope, like the woman at the well, we can sit across from Jesus and let him open our eyes to our patterns and dependence, so that we, too, can confidently walk into what God has called us to.

Before attending that luncheon and hearing that talk with my husband, I'd never truly stopped to see my own destructive patterns. I had held the hands of those who victimized me, and in a sense, had victimized myself. Deep down, I believed God's love was true for everyone except me, which led me to search for more love elsewhere. I was looking for water to quench my thirst in all the wrong places. I avoided facing the patterns that put wedges between me, God, and his purpose for my life.

My dependency on man only grew more harmful until I named it for what it was. Time didn't heal me, but in time, I began to heal because I changed what I depended upon.

God desires to meet us in the same way he met the woman at the well. He leaves the ninety-nine for the lost one, to bring us back to his safety.[5] He seeks to show us our unhealthy dependencies so we can fully depend on him. He knows we will not find fulfillment in others or in ourselves, but points to ultimate fulfillment through himself. Then, when he calls us into his ministry and mission—the way he did with the woman at the well—we do not go preaching what we do not know. Rather, we go as witnesses of his life-changing, radical, pattern-calling-out, thirst-quenching love.

LIE 6

YOUR FEELINGS
ARE NOT VALID

WHEN I GRADUATED FROM HIGH SCHOOL, I WAS ECSTATIC
to run track in college. I ended high school as a four-time state
champion in track and field, and I felt like I was just beginning
my track career. Competing in this capacity was how I would
run the race marked out for me.[1]

I first met my college coach, Coach Ron, at an all-star meet
after I had won State. He frantically followed me around during my warm-up and cooldown, spoke to me rapidly and loudly
about the amazing school he was recruiting for, and boasted
about how he had trained Olympians. I could be an Olympian,
too, he said. After the meet, Coach Ron called multiple times
a day until I made a firm commitment to run for him. I was
flattered by his bombastic pursuit of me and belief in my talent
and hard work. I told myself and him often that I did not want

to waste the gift of running that God had given me by drinking, being lazy, or failing to give each practice my absolute best, which made him excited to train together.

Though I ran short-distance races in high school, including the 100-meter dash and 200-meter dash, Coach Ron said I was "tough enough" to add the 400-meter dash to my competitions and training. While that might have been a relatively easy transition for most sprinters going from high school to college, my coach also had me competing in cross-country because the women who were actually supposed to run cross-country were injured. I know now but did not realize then that they were injured because of our coach's training. I didn't argue or question my coach's authority; he'd said listening to him was what I had to do to be the best athlete I could possibly be. But after a few months of training in college, my legs were in immense pain. I even felt a tingling feeling when I ran. At some practices I would cry and fall to the ground, which had never happened to me in a practice before. When you touched my shins and calves, they felt hard, as if rock was underneath my skin.

No matter how much pain I appeared to be in or what I told my coach, he said I was being weak and simply needed to gain strength. On top of that, he told me I was too skinny and needed to gain weight. Then, when I followed his orders, he told me months later that I had gained too much weight and now needed to lose it. Suddenly, I struggled with disordered eating. On a full-ride track scholarship, I felt like I had no room to question him. Track was the means to pay for the education my mom and I had always wanted for me.

He continued training one-on-one with me, more than he did with any of my teammates, all on top of adding a sport my body was not made for. Then, right in the middle of my first college indoor track season, the college opened an investigation on Coach Ron. I didn't know why, but through email, the team was made aware that Coach was abruptly banned from practices. Despite the ban, soon after that email was sent, Coach Ron sent me a text. He still wanted to pick me up and drive me off campus daily so we could practice together.

During our training time off campus, he would tell me what to say if anyone asked me questions about his training. Unaware that he was manipulating me, I actually thought what he said sounded right. I felt very special to be the only one practicing with him and believed it was because he thought I was especially talented. This is the perfect example of how trauma affects our minds and relationships, tricking us into coming closer to people who hurt us as we search for validation.

By the time I arrived home that summer, I did not like running and my legs hurt even when running short distances. I would lie on the track, dreading another set of practice blocks. The sport that used to be my greatest joy had become the nightmare I shook myself to wake up from.

That same summer, I received a call telling me that my college coach was fired. Some of my teammates, who were far more aware than I, had gone to administration about the coach's misconduct. Though I did understand that something was wrong, I didn't have the words or context to describe what was happening to me—but my teammates called it "athlete abuse" and "misconduct." The feelings I had about training with Coach Ron were shoved down so I could grow tough enough, get stronger, continue my education, and maintain the relationship we had, even if it wasn't the healthiest. So many of us shove our feelings down because that's what we've learned to do to survive.

Though the toxic situation was laid out for me more clearly than before, when my college coach contacted me again that summer, he claimed that the real problem was my teammates' laziness. I, he said, did not have the same problems as them because I worked hard. He said if I wanted to continue to succeed, I needed to follow him to wherever he would coach next. Though I knew his training was not helping me excel as an athlete, his continued compliments and validation—things I did not receive as a child—convinced me that the best choice for my college career was to follow him. So I decided to transfer wherever he went.

Every summer during college, I went home to my adoptive dad, who was also my high school track coach. When I had a hard decision to make, my dad, Scott, always said the right words, which I hope to say to my own kids when they begin to make hard decisions. To this very day, my dad tells me, "I know you will make the right decision. You always do."

His words were powerful because, whenever I heard them, they prompted me to make a good decision. His belief in me spurred me on to do what was right more times than not. He tried his best to be a good listener and limit his input. I now know he did this because when he did say something, his words would hold great weight. This strategy worked well.

While my dad is not someone to give much advice, but rather one to wait until I make a decision and then support me throughout it, he began to warn me against following Coach Ron. During the time I was considering a transfer, several other college coaches were reaching out and offering me full-ride scholarships. I think my adoptive dad and I both realized how much stock I put in the hands of authority figures and how much I needed someone to steer me clear of another year of pain and agony. Even when my eyes were opened to reality, I needed someone else with authority to reassure me in whatever decision I made because I never felt like I could trust myself. I sought everyone else's assurance for clarity. So after hearing out my dad, I decided not to follow Coach Ron but transfer to a different college.

Still, months after I transferred colleges—and despite having a different coach, significantly better training, and a healthier environment—my legs hurt. This led me to many doctors' appointments and medical tests that left my questions unanswered. As hard as the sport had become, I loved it and my teammates. I didn't want to stop running, so I ran through the pain and continued to see doctors. After so many appointments, I finally found myself in the office of a specialist who diagnosed me with compartment syndrome due to my first college coach's training. I then had to get an immediate surgery that left four massive scars on both of my legs.

I share this because relationships and stories like these were recurring in my life—all because I ignored many of my own instincts and feelings. I rationalized the unhealthy dynamics over and over again by saying I was "dying to myself" and "suffering for the glory of God." I'd stay in relationships preaching "love never fails," but in reality, I had a deep yearning for affirmation and validation from significant others and authority figures. I depended on the opinions of people to fill me until they failed me, which they always did—not because all people are bad, but because all people are not God.

Unfortunately, this problem was compounded by a message I heard in church: that feelings aren't facts, and I should not listen to my feelings. Whenever I did feel uneasy or question the toxicity of a relationship, I questioned my own judgment too. There were plenty of moments when my feelings were pointing me to health and holiness, but I questioned them too much to act. I named my feelings false and validated others' words instead.

This book was born out of a searing desire to understand why I made such choices. I had to answer the questions, How could I have such great intentions to love, yet also have this pattern of brokenness in my relationships? How could I attempt to obtain the confidence of the Lord yet be so insecure in myself and in every decision I make?

CODEPENDENT NO MORE

When my husband struggled with alcoholism, I sat down to do some research on how to fix his unhealthy dependence on alcohol. I googled, read books from experts, and found articles from those who had recovered. As I read more and more, I began to tilt my head and wonder if I had my own troubling problem to deal with—mainly because the research was telling me that those who struggle with addiction commonly have partners who are unhealthily dependent on them. While trying to fix him, I discovered that the greater piece that needed to be fixed was me.

In other words, I was indeed codependent.

According to Mental Health America, codependency "is an emotional and behavioral condition that affects an individual's ability to have healthy, mutually satisfying relationships." Codependency was actually first brought to light when psychologists observed the families of alcoholics and the unhealthy behaviors and dynamics within those who surrounded them. A codependent often enables another person's destructive behavior regardless of how it hurts them and others. In a sense, codependent people seek out and are addicted to relationships because relationships seem to validate their self-worth.[2]

If I had to describe codependency simply, I would say it is an unhealthy dependence on people rather than a healthy dependence on God. And I had it.

When we are reliant on other people's opinions and guidance, we're like feathers in the wind—susceptible to any gust that comes along. When someone makes us feel unwanted, we try harder and commit to doing what they suggest even more. We become so accustomed to this pattern that we prioritize the voice of man—and God ends up not having much of a say in our lives as a result. It is difficult to feel his presence or hear his whispers, because when we are codependent we give others power over how we feel rather than giving God our attention.

As Christians, codependency can be especially hard to discern when we are told to seek wise counsel and submit to governing authorities because our hearts are deceitful and desperately sick.[3] Taken out of context and taught by people with ulterior motives, these maxims can cause us to distrust the intimate ways God can speak to us—leading us to trust the wrong people instead. It may even be evident that we have put our trust in people who are hurting us, but it is easier to think of ourselves as the ones at fault. From here, we end up in broken relationships and learn not to trust ourselves even more. We are left feeling insecure about our intuition, and we again are urged to seek validation from those who hurt us.

My codependency and heavy reliance on others stemmed from not knowing my value. I had also muted my internal compass. When we question our value and identity, we hand them over for others to determine. This is especially scary when those people are not healthy themselves—because if they cannot have a right view of themselves, they will struggle to have a right view of others. You can't expect someone to be right about who you are when they can't even be honest about who they are. As codependent people we look to others to understand who we are, what we should do, and how we should *feel* because we are not secure in our innate, God-given worth. Ultimately, when we battle codependent tendencies and patterns, we struggle to feel anything for ourselves because we feel so much on behalf of others.

These patterns I'm talking about are subtle. They can be difficult to identify, and we shouldn't be too hard on ourselves for not seeing them sooner. At the same time, it is helpful to acknowledge that we cannot beg God to heal us while staying loyal to the patterns that hurt us.

> We cannot beg God to heal us while staying loyal to the patterns that hurt us.

So what do we do? How do we start to understand and value our own feelings and instincts instead of looking to others to tell us how to feel? First, let's look at some lies we believe about feelings. We tend to view feelings in two extremes: The first perspective is that feelings are leaders, and however we feel is true. The second is that feelings are bad, and we must shove them down so they do not lead us astray. Neither perspective honors our feelings, which God has given us and which Jesus Christ had too. Making our feelings our leaders gives them too much control and drowns out God's voice, while disregarding feelings boxes out God from speaking to us and silences the Holy Spirit moving.

This thought pattern changed in me when I was given permission by a therapist to think of my feelings in a new way. My feelings are not God's voice, and they are not my sole controller, but they are guides and indicators that lead me to ask myself and God questions. One of the ways I began to heal from codependency was to begin to feel feelings again, not only when they were extreme but in my everyday ordinary life. In smaller ways, I let my feelings guide me, until I learned to become more comfortable with them guiding me in bigger decisions.

As children we are supposed to learn from our caregivers how to regulate our emotions, but if it wasn't taught or modeled to us, the lesson can be much more difficult to learn in our adult years. Thankfully, it is not too late to learn our feelings and emotions. People who struggle with codependency and those who come from traumatic backgrounds often feel emotions in extremes. We either shove them down or feel them in ways that are overwhelming and more striking than those who grew up in more stable and healthy families. It can be difficult to identify an emotion in the latter situation, because the emotion often comes to us in the form of a reaction. However, these extremes can be balanced as we learn to understand the ways God speaks to us and learn to trust our intuition and feelings when he does speak. This happens bit by bit, as we ask good questions and take small actions to begin trusting the little God-whisper inside.

Here are some questions we can ask God as we learn to let him guide our feelings:

- "Why do I feel this way?"
- "Is this feeling legitimate? What evidence do I see that validates this feeling?"
- "How could this feeling guide me toward the truth?"
- "What might you have to say about me feeling this way, God?"

These questions can guide us toward what is good. They can help us begin to listen to ourselves and put stock in our own God-given intuition over the voices of others. These questions can slowly unravel us from codependency in relationships and lead us toward depending on the voice of God. If we spend years believing that our feelings are not valid, we don't learn how to trust the different ways God has created us to hear him. But when we do begin to trust ourselves, our feelings can become sails that blow us away from dependency outside of God and toward a genuine dependence on him.

TO FEEL AGAIN

When my firstborn was still in the womb, a middle-aged mom and church woman took me under her wing. I soaked up every piece of advice I could from her. I believe it was her faith that drew me toward her and influenced me to trust nearly everything she said.

Believing that there was only a small chance I could be a good mom, and insecure because of my own upbringing, I believed I needed to take in and apply every ounce of advice I received from Kimberly. But eventually I started taking in her insults, hurtful jabs, and "advice" about my motherhood, my past, and my character because I wanted to meet the standards she said would make a good Christian wife, mom, and woman. Anything she endorsed, I strived to become. I wanted to please her as if she were my own mother, and I hoped she would fill a maternal role in my life.

As I yearned for Kimberly's pride in her motherhood to transform to pride in me, our relationship spiraled out of control. We'd take biweekly trips to Costco together, where she'd nitpick at what I'd say, not say, or do. I usually struggled to process what she said until I was alone. Her words felt like parasites crawling from my brain to my gut, and once they got there, my emotions became word vomit. I didn't have the coping skills to express my emotions appropriately or determine that much of what she said was based on her own insecurity and pain—so I'd lash out in long, verbally abusive text messages.

This experience taught me that my patterns in relationships with boys in high school and college did not change much at all after marriage. I thought marriage would solve my issues, but it only magnified them, forcing me to look at how my unhealthy patterns transferred from one type of person to another. The same unhealthy cycles I thought I'd escaped went from being centered around my mom to the young men I dated to a middle-aged woman at my church. This taught me that if we don't deal with our trauma, the way it manifests will transfer one way or another. From person to person or from dependency to dependency, trauma will find a way to keep hurting us if we don't find a way to heal from it.

I thought I had to pursue people who did not and could not show me love to prove myself lovable. I had to become whatever they found most acceptable to show myself I was worth accepting.

At times I've struggled to discern what truth is despite knowing *the* truth. This struggle seems to be common among people who have experienced deep grief or trauma, and especially among those who struggle to trust their own feelings or intuition. One day, in my quiet time, I read 2 Timothy 3:6–7, where Paul said there are people who "worm their way into homes and gain control over gullible women . . . always learning but never able to come to a knowledge of the truth." Some translations change the word *gullible* to *weak* or *silly*,[4] but the original root of the Greek word *gynaikaria* is *gymna*, which translates to "exposed" or "naked."[5] In the English language *vulnerable* is a synonym of *exposed*, and it is true that some of us are more vulnerable to codependent relationships where people "worm their way in" because we have been overexposed.

People who struggle with codependent tendencies—especially those who have experienced trauma or have felt alone or abandoned—often ignore their own needs in hopes of pleasing others enough so they will stay. Shame and questions of self-worth continue to pile upon us when people leave or when we don't become exactly what others want us to become.

Whether you are an orphan, a survivor of childhood trauma, or a sufferer in any other way, heartbreaks can leave you more raw and exposed. In codependent relationship patterns, we often give more than we should, sometimes more than anyone asked; become what others want us to be; and take on others' opinions and beliefs as our own. Like a person giving layers of clothes off their back until they are left with nothing, we give up our talents, gifts, and beliefs until we feel like we have nothing left. In turn, and in attempts to gain security, we seek out relationships—people to protect us—who are willing to give it all to undo what has been done. We hope they will reclothe us, not realizing that the cycle is only continuing. Our overexposure leaves us vulnerable to false teachings and lies again and again. Our unguarded hearts allow for anything and anyone to have what should be God's, even when we sense we should move toward something different.

The way out of this deep insecurity is to seek God through his Word and be selective about wise counsel. By listening to his life-giving voice, we can confidently take back our sense of self from people and hand it back to God, who holds it firmly and unwaveringly as we hold on to the tail of our Father's robe.

SAYING NO IS NOT SELFISH

A couple of years ago, my husband and I received a call to take in a foster-care placement who would almost immediately become adoptable. Their biological parents' rights had been terminated, and they were being removed from their prospective adoptive family because, sadly, the prospective adoptive family was abusive. My husband and I have a heart for adoption, and the phone call excited us—but in this season, we were at capacity. At times we had said yes to too many responsibilities, had failed the people in front of us, and had learned from our mistakes. Now, the responsibilities we wanted to steward well were the ones in front of us, and they were already showing us how limited we were.

However, these were real kids, God's kids, who needed a loving, permanent family, and we could possibly be that for them. In my gut, I felt like the answer was no. I believed another family could also offer them the love, time, and attention they needed, and in that season, I felt it wasn't us—but to say no felt so selfish.

I called my mentor Danielle, described the turmoil I was feeling, and expressed that I didn't know what to do. She prayed for me, asked me good questions as she always did, and reminded me to keep my eyes on God. And then she said, "The flesh is selfish, but the self is sacred." I was pacing, but those words stopped me in my tracks, reassured my gut feeling, and gave me the answer I needed. Danielle gave me permission to see myself not as a wretch who was inherently selfish, but as a saint, made new, who could make the right decision with the Holy Spirit. Before these words, I thought my sinful nature was prompting me to say no to those kids. I assumed I was being selfish, but in reality, saying no to them was saying yes to being selfless, loving, and attentive to my work, to the kids already in my home, and to the other people God had called me to right then and there. I sure do hope we can adopt someday but that was not the right time for us, and I needed to hear Danielle's words that day. And since then, her words have helped me make many similarly hard decisions— and I hope they will help guide you too.

Accepting that my feelings were not invalid took a lot

of practice. There were many relationships I had to distance myself from and people I simply had to stop listening to. Because I viewed myself as so lowly, I'd allowed many other voices to trump nearly every gut feeling I had. I took advice from people who did not know me well and people who didn't practice what they preached. I believed I needed that help to "be better." But when I challenged myself to discern the voices in my life alongside the Holy Spirit's voice, I started prioritizing people who genuinely knew me and who were living lives that bore fruit.

Now, let me be clear: When we limit the voices in our lives, we should not just pick the ones that agree with us or appease our agendas. We want to trust the voices that spur us toward fulfilling God's agenda. As time went on, I became better at not only knowing what wise counsel to listen to but also at hearing the voice of God on my own. The microphones in our lives cannot be given to anyone who wants to tell us where to be, when to be there, who to be, and how to be it. God's voice must be the loudest. With enough practice, we'll begin to trust the small whisper and gentle feeling that is our Guide. When we get a feeling in the pit of our stomachs about right and wrong but someone else tries to contradict that feeling, we must remember the truth: God *does* speak to us through our feelings and not all of them are leading us astray. We can learn to feel again, knowing that some of our strongest feelings lead us right back to God.

LIE 7

YOU HAVE TO DEFEND YOURSELF

IN THE 1920S PSYCHOLOGIST WALTER BRADFORD Cannon coined the term *fight or flight* to describe an evolutionary survival mechanism.[1] He was referring to automatic, nearly uncontrollable responses to danger meant to assist humans in overcoming a threat. But to many trauma survivors, the fight-or-flight response can become unhelpful, sometimes harmful, and hard to turn off. Many people who have been through trauma have an overactive trauma response, so they get stuck in the reactions of fight, flight, freeze, or fawn. This is called *hypervigilance*, and it stems from being raised in unsafe, unpredictable, and chaotic environments.[2]

When I was a preteen my mom started receiving disability checks and staying home, which put us in each other's vicinity more than ever before, especially during the summer months.

We fought a lot when we moved to the trailer park. Before that, her ex-husband and her long workdays had acted as a buffer between us, but since her divorce and a car accident that took her out of work, our circumstances had changed.

Mom would yell, and when I couldn't take it anymore, I would yell back. She often accused me of stealing when she lost her belongings, typically her keys or her wallet. Though I never stole those items, I occasionally stole four quarters out of the change jar to walk to the convenience store at the end of the trailer park, appropriately named ShortStop, to buy myself a bag of Flamin' Hot Cheetos.

Every opportunity to leave, I took. I was twelve at this point, and Mom's manic episodes overwhelmed me. Sometimes I would scream with no words, just wails, so I could drown out the accusations and name-calling. Then she'd scream, "Get out!" And I never had to be told twice. She'd run after me, from one end of the trailer to the other, regretting her words right after she said them, but I was fast enough to get away and jump out the back door of our brown-and-white tin home. I'd run, filled with fear that Mom would get in the car and come after me, moving my legs as fast as I could for about two hundred meters to the end of the trailer park road, past the brick apartment complex, toward my friend Bridget's house.

It was a relief to plop down on Bridget's bed. I am not sure why she lived with her grandparents, but kids with dysfunctional families find homes in one another, literally and figuratively, so there I was. Though neither of us could put what we went through into words, we understood each other.

Within about thirty minutes, Bridget's grandparents received a call to their landline. My stomach dropped when it rang. I assumed it was my mom, but to my surprise it was the police labeling me a "runaway" and threatening to press charges against me for unruliness. The same mom who told me to leave called the police and then came to pick me up. She'd sit and talk with Bridget's grandparents, mastering her ability to mask the abuse in our home with sad musings like, "She doesn't have a father."

As our fights continued, I kept running. To parks. To the mall. Anywhere that shielded my ears from hearing her. One evening I ran to a playground an acre or two across from our trailer park. There were many enclosures, like tube slides or a wooden beehive, where kids could easily go unnoticed during a game of hide-and-seek. I had planned to stay the night in one of them and go to school the next morning, but I think Mom knew I never went far. Soon after a report from Mom, a policeman picked me up from the park. As I sat in the back of the police car for the short drive home, the officer said, "You are continuing to be a problem for us. If you run away again, I'll have to take you out to jail." There again, an adult spoke the narrative over me that I was the problem. That narrative played a large part in my questioning whether my sanity was intact. It caused me to question myself for years to come.

The police officer walked me up to the porch. The door flung open, and Mom—wearing a plush robe, playing the damsel in distress, and saying she was so glad I was okay—hugged me in between her thanks to the officer.

Considering Mom's manipulation tactics, and since jail was the next stop, I was forced to change my survival mode from flight to fight. Easy enough. There has always been a fighter in me—from slapping a girl on the bus who made fun of me for living in a trailer park to sticking up for Mom when the men she dated called her mean slurs.

My transition between survival mechanisms was not intentional, but I can see how it came so naturally to me. So the next time Mom hurt me, I hit her back. But I did not stop. I kept hitting her.

I'll never forget hitting Mom—the deep regret I felt afterward. When I tell people the story, they have sympathy for me and say, "It was self-defense." Though it may have started that way, it continued out of a rage buried in me. I'd hurt Mom the same way she hurt me, and that scared me. I would have preferred to run.

Ironically, after Mom called the cops, a policeman arrived that night, put me in handcuffs, and took me to the juvenile detention center I was trying to avoid.

Weeks later when we went to court, the truth about my homelife was revealed, and I entered the foster-care system for the second time in my life. Naturally, as a teenage girl hoping to be accepted by the new people who took me in, my survival mechanism went from flight to fawn. The fawn response is a lesser-known survival mechanism in which an individual tries to avoid or minimize distress or danger by pleasing and appeasing the perceived threat.[3] Fawning was the conditioned practice I thought would keep me safe.

Fawning doesn't seem that bad when you're doing it. It actually doesn't seem bad at all, especially as a Christian. We are taught as Christians to die to ourselves. We are taught to put others before ourselves and meet others' needs even when it costs us.[4] We can very easily be fawning while covering it up with biblical principles like kindness, patience, and gentleness.

As a teenager, I did not know fawning had become my way of survival. What could ever be wrong with making everyone so well pleased with me? I never suspected there could be another side to this tactic. From flight to fight to fawn to feeling like I'd lost my sense of self and the whereabouts of my God.

LOOKING FOR A DEFENDER

My relationship with my mom was broken from the age of nine. It wasn't necessarily the beatings that shattered our bond, but her words that dove into my brain and infused themselves into my memory. The verbal abuse Mom put me through damaged my identity and my view of myself, much more than any number of blows did.

Despite that, I'd forgive Mom because I understood Christ forgave me. I loved Mom and still do because I know she did her very best, but despite both of our very bests, our relationship never mended like I'd hoped.

I yearned for a relationship with my mom like the ones described in fantastical social media posts—the kinds of maternal relationships that seemed fictional but were real. I wanted a mom I could "tell everything to" because she would actually listen. I wanted a mom who would call me her best friend and I'd call her mine.

When I was about to become a mom myself for the first time, the church lady Kimberly gave me hope for that kind of relationship. She was almost a decade older than my mom, she had a handful of adult children following Jesus, she was a leader in the church, and she spouted impressive taglines like "I was born with confidence" and "God gave me the gift of faith." It all looked good to me. I knew God was laying down a path for me to walk in ministry, so I leaned in and sought her guidance and mentorship. As we grew closer in our relationship, she'd casually say, "I see you and love you like a daughter." That meant a whole lot more to me than we both realized. I clung to the idea that I could be like her daughter. Neither she nor I understood how heavy those words sat with me until she and her biological daughter went on a girls' trip, and I looked at their smiling faces in photos on social media and started wallowing and wondering why I was not invited.

In the beginning of my relationship with Kimberly, I initiated spending a lot of time with her. I think a part of me actually did want to spend time with her, but I know now that a greater part of me wanted the time to prove to her that I was good enough to be a daughter to her.

When we are unhealed we can find offense in anything— and with hindsight, I understand that I was easily offended *and* that she targeted me in ways that presumably had to do with her own trauma and insecurity.

Nonetheless, I would grow tired of pleasing her and speak up to defend my character, positions, and values. Usually what started as an attempt to clarify myself turned into me insulting her in return. I simply meant to defend myself, but it all too easily turned unkind and harsh. I fought. Relentlessly. Sometimes righteously and sometimes unjustifiably, but more than anything I was fighting for the mother I'd always wanted. I was fighting to feel a little more whole, less broken, and more loved.

After so many times of clinging to Kimberly, receiving insults, exploding, leaving, and clinging again, I took a long break from her by not speaking with her in any form. I was attempting to escape the toxicity, but then Kimberly would reach out. She'd claim that my not engaging in the relationship and conflict demonstrated that I lacked bravery and the ability to have hard conversations. These words hurt me greatly. I had taken a step back to heal, not only because she'd hurt me but also because I'd hurt her.

But I'd reenter the relationship with the codependent patterns of apologizing profusely, feeling even more obligated to be who she wanted me to be, and wanting to show her that I could have hard conversations and be brave. What hurt the most was that she always pointed back to my upbringing to prove our issues were really *my* issues—just like my mom when I held the knife to my neck and just like the cop who never asked what my homelife was like. I returned to that relationship fearing that if I couldn't make it right, I would be living proof of my greatest fear—that I was the problem all along.

Since that time I've cried out many prayers asking why God did not give me my fairy-tale ending and grant me the mother I'd hoped for. I've written many words that will never be read. I've spoken countless words to therapists. And I've read many verses that have brought peace to my stirring heart and answers to my questions. One of those was Psalm 28:7, written by King David. I imagine David saying these words, half-heartedly feeling them, and hoping that where his mouth went, his heart would eventually follow. I envision David, like me, with tears running down his face, yearning for people to see him fairly. He said, "The LORD protects and defends me; I trust in him. He gives me help and makes me glad; I praise him with joyful songs" (GNT).

Most of my outbursts at Kimberly came amid my attempts to defend myself. I so badly wished she would change the way she saw me. In this psalm, David was crying out to God about wicked men in his life who were judging him and bringing others to judge him. He was crying out to be heard because his self-defense had been silenced.

Before saying much of anything else in this prayer, David addressed God as his Defender. This scripture inspired me to make God's name on my lips the same; and even when I didn't believe the words of that verse applied to me, reciting them helped my faith move a centimeter toward the belief that God truly *was* my Defender. So I kept believing and saying and praying and singing, "God, my Defender." This new mantra took me out of a pattern of defending myself to survive and taught me that God himself would defend me.

David had known God as his Defender from a young age. It is assumed that David was between thirteen and fifteen when he went to battle with a giant that many doubted he would defeat.[5] In response to their doubt, David said, "The LORD who rescued me from the paw of the lion and the paw of the bear will rescue me from the hand of this Philistine."[6] David saw God as the one who fought with him and for him. God surely was with David when he defeated Goliath. And God surely is with us in our battles.

> God surely is with us in our battles.

GOD IS MY DEFENDER

After not speaking to Kimberly for another round of months, temptation would ping me to send the text message, to prove my character, to defend my position—to go back to the survival mechanism of fighting. But this time, I just paused and chose to believe that God was defending me with better words, visions, insights, and dreams than I could ever conjure on my own. God saw me for who I truly was, and he'd defend me in the unseen.

I've identified myself as a "survivor" for years now, but by this time in my life, I had to admit that my survival mechanisms had proved themselves ultimately inadequate for mending this relationship. I had to trade my sword of worldly survival for the belief that God was fighting on my behalf even when I couldn't see, hear, or feel it. The fighter in me used to stand in front of God, swinging aimlessly until I lost my strength and stamina. But that's not sustainable. When I took myself out of the vicious cycle of defending myself, started stepping back and being quiet until I finally caught my breath, I finally found peace. And I finally found strength after feeling weary for so long.

If you, too, are trying to catch your breath, reclaim your peace, and gain back strength, I invite you to reevaluate your survival mechanisms, take my mantras, and speak them over yourself: *God knows the real me. He will defend me. God is my Defender.*

May these words replace the constant fight of proving ourselves because they remind us that God is always fighting for us.

Second Corinthians 10:3–4 says, "Though we live in the world, we do not wage war as the world does. The weapons we fight with are not the weapons of the world. On the contrary, they have divine power to demolish strongholds." We fight with the weapons of God, and many times that means holding our tongue, being kind anyway, and letting God defend us.

If you're someone who can't fathom not confronting someone when they have mischaracterized you, consider Proverbs 23:9–11: "Do not speak to fools, for they will scorn your prudent words. Do not move an ancient boundary stone or encroach on the fields of the fatherless, for their Defender is strong." And remember Exodus 14:14: "The Lord will fight for you; you need only to be still." You and I have a strong Defender when we declare God is the one who can fight for us.

The fighter in us has to learn how to take a step behind Christ: the soldier of truth and a warrior for his children. He is our sword, and we only need to hold on—not swing, not stab. He is fighting on our behalf with the perfect amount of anger, with precise aim, for all the right reasons, in all the right ways so we don't have to. He is our Defender.

LIE 8

THERE IS SOMETHING WRONG WITH YOU

AS AN ADULT I WENT TO MY MOM AND ASKED HER IF SHE remembered beating me as a child. She usually responded with, "Of course! You deserved it."

Many of the people who have hurt you and me were likely not aware of the ways they hurt us. This could mean that we also do not know how we are hurting others—a fear that haunts those of us who do not want to hurt others the same way we have been hurt.

Trying to be meticulously self-aware was my antidote to this fear. I thought if I could be keenly aware of myself, I wouldn't hurt people. If I could figure out my fault in any conflict, then I could control what needed to be fixed in the situation. But if it was not clear what needed to be fixed—even in situations I wasn't involved in—I imagined that someone had finally found the piece in me that was wrong, and it probably looked a lot like my abuser. Believing that there was a piece of me that I was unaware of, a piece that did the kind of damage that was done to me, something damaging, made me so anxious—sometimes so crushingly anxious I thought it would be easier to not exist.

As Christians, we tend to expect goodwill to come our way if we control our thoughts, think positively, and treat people right. Nonetheless, pieces of my brain and body simply remained fractured in fear, and my fear's favorite escape was thoughts of suicide.

I understand this is a taboo topic to discuss, especially in a Christian book, but I've chosen to talk about suicide because our brains can take us there when we're stuck in toxic cyclical thought patterns. I also understand that Christian leaders are expected to appear nearly flawless—an expectation that perpetuates toxic thoughts, mental illness, and suicidal ideation. And I know I'm not able to live a perfect life. I don't even want to, so I am choosing to live openly and talk about it. Too many of us are scared of being counted out of what we wish to be qualified for, so we stay silent. Too many of us are afraid of being labeled insane, so we keep our suicidal thoughts a secret. But as I've opened up about my own struggle with these thoughts, I have found that others face the same—and when they hear someone who gets to do what I do speaking honestly, they feel like maybe they aren't so broken after all.

THERE IS SOMETHING RIGHT WITH YOU

Suicidal ideation has been a thorn in my side since I was about twelve years old. The thoughts started because suicide felt like the only solution to escape Mom's yelling when I couldn't leave the house. As I got older, it felt like the only way to silence the curses that were embedded in my mind—curses that originated with my mom. I fantasized less about suicide as I got older, but these thoughts never completely went away. I prayed. I was in community. I read Scripture. But the idea of dying still came. Sometimes the thoughts still emerge today.

I say this so you'll know you aren't alone in the darkness of your mind. I am there with you. Very likely, many others are too. But it's easy to feel like you are struggling alone with these thoughts.

There's a theological framework called the *prosperity gospel* that is a bit controversial across Christian denominations. If you have never heard the term, the prosperity gospel purports that if you do good deeds, work hard, pray harder, believe the hardest, and do not think or speak anything negative, you will live a prosperous life. Many would say you wouldn't have suicidal thoughts or struggle with mental illness either. With the right religious practices and the holiest of thoughts, the prosperity gospel promises financial abundance, minimal to no suffering, and healthy bodies and brains.

This theology shames us for our hurt. This theology says, "If you're hurting, you are far from God." Even though Psalm 34:18 says, "The Lord is close to the brokenhearted and saves those who are crushed in spirit." When we believe the former, we shy away from pain and suffering, or we cover it up by putting on a happy mask. This contradicts not only the Christian faith but Jesus himself, whose greatest act of glorifying God was to suffer on the cross. Mental illness does not always equate with a lack of faith or indicate something is wrong with us.

Sometimes our mental health issues mean we have a thorn in our flesh persistently pricking us. That thorn points to the truth that we aren't gods but mere humans with God dwelling among us.

In 2 Corinthians 12:7–9, Paul said, "In order to keep me from becoming conceited, I was given a thorn in my flesh, a messenger of Satan, to torment me. Three times I pleaded with the Lord to take it away from me. But he said to me, 'My grace is sufficient for you, for my power is made perfect in weakness.' Therefore I will boast all the more gladly about my weaknesses, so that Christ's power may rest on me."

We can see that Paul did not remain silent about his own thorn—his suffering. Paul voiced his pain. He embraced his weaknesses, and his words make those of us who have a thorn feel a little more human. We, as Christians, are Jesus' modern-day disciples, and when we look at Paul as an apostle and disciple, we see an example of one who did not remain silent about his struggles. He was honest about them.

This is important to consider because Paul was a missionary who helped many people—one of the first ever to preach to Gentiles that they were saved by their faith in Christ and not by good deeds. He gave us a blueprint for what it looks like to spread the gospel. Some would say Paul is the most important person after Jesus in the history of Christianity, yet like us, he wasn't disqualified because of his thorn.

Though we do not know exactly what Paul's thorn was, some scholars believe that Paul was suicidal because of the words he wrote in Philippians 1:21–26:

> For to me, to live is Christ and to die is gain. If I am to go on living in the body, this will mean fruitful labor for me. Yet what shall I choose? I do not know! I am torn between the two: I desire to depart and be with Christ, which is better by far; but it is more necessary for you that I remain in the body. Convinced of this, I know that I will remain, and I will continue with all of you for your progress and joy in the faith, so that through my being with you again your boasting in Christ Jesus will abound on account of me.[1]

It is sad to think about where we would be had Paul chosen to "depart." It is necessary that you remain in the body, as God has a specific purpose and plan for your life, like he had for Paul. To help many people. To spread the gospel through the gifts he has given you. To love others and to be loved.

Those of us with broken brains and suicidal thoughts can be comforted by the thorn and thoughts Paul dealt with. Paul was so great that if he boasted, what he said about himself would be true. So God gave him a thorn in his side, an issue to struggle with continually, so Paul would not bring glory unto himself but bring all the glory to God. It was necessary for Paul to have a weakness so God's strength would shine through. Maybe the thorn you deal with is not because something is wrong with you but because there is something right with you—and in the gifts God has given you, you can rejoice in your weakness because that is where God's strength reveals itself.

IF SOMEONE STRUGGLES WITH SUICIDE OR MENTAL HEALTH

In Isaiah 53:3 Jesus is described as a man of suffering who is familiar with pain. He was known by his troubles. His struggles were his constant companions and familiar acquaintances from the cradle to the cross. The scripture also says that people hid their faces from him, despised him, and even held him in low esteem. Sadly, in the church we have sometimes done the same to those who struggle with suicidal ideation and mental health challenges.

During a season of desperation, I expressed to church leaders that I was struggling to navigate my trauma, which led me to have immense anxiety. Some of the heartrending responses sounded like,

- "Just trust in God."
- "God is not wringing his hands over this."
- "You are letting the devil have a foothold."
- "You need to pray more."

John Welwood was known as a Buddhist teacher and psychotherapist who would refer to these responses as *spiritual bypassing*. He coined the term in the 1980s and described it as a "tendency to use spiritual ideas and practices to sidestep or avoid facing unresolved emotional issues, psychological wounds, and unfinished developmental tasks."[2] When using this term he was actually referring to his Buddhist community, but this kind of avoidance of hard situations is also prevalent in the Christian church. Spiritual bypassing plagues many religions, and unfortunately it leaves us spiritually immature. To truly be mature in the faith—if we want the church to be a safe place and if we want to heal—we should acknowledge our emotions.

I know there are countless others who have received responses like these, so if you haven't heard this already, let me tell you that these pat answers are *not* reflections of the heart of God. God weeps alongside us. He holds us and cares deeply about our pain. He does not turn us away in our hurt. He embraces us. Our communities should do the same, and we should do the same for others.

During times when I have struggled and heard responses like these, my thoughts only became worse and began to consume me. I would think, *My faith is trash, and my relationship with God is void because of my mental health.* My greatest fear was that if I wasn't "good enough" in my faith, I would lose my relationship with God altogether—but I didn't want to tell anyone else about the thoughts I was struggling with because I was afraid the confession would only point to me being a bad

Christian. Many Christians remain quiet about their mental health for the same reasons.

I did a survey at my home church and on social media, asking other Christians who were active in church communities from all over the country why they did not share their mental health struggles with anyone in the church. Here are some of their answers:

> "When I did share it was always insinuated that if I just had 'enough faith' I wouldn't be anxious and depressed, but no matter how much I prayed I still felt sad. I always felt like a bad Christian."
>
> —BECKY

> "I did decide to share about my anxiety, and even in my fairly reasonable and supportive family it was suggested as an 'issue of faith.'"
>
> —ANNA

> "It was suggested that God is supposed to be enough and my joy should come from him. That made me think if I am sad, maybe I don't have God after all, and that's a really scary thought that in turn made me more sad."
>
> —OLIVIA

There were hundreds of responses very similar to these. When so many people testify in this way, it's time to acknowledge we have an issue in church culture at large.

This culture depends on a toxic narrative that if one is hurting or suffering, they must not *know* God. In turn, instead of living honestly with one another, we stuff our hurt deep down. This leaves churches feeling less connected, compassionate, or empathetic. Then, when hiding our pain, we lose out on key characteristics of Christ, the main one being how he suffered.

Reaching out to community and leaders in the church ought to be helpful. But these responses felt like someone taking a chipping tool to my faith. When I heard these responses, my relationship with God felt like crumbled concrete in my hands. The one thing I'd always been sure would bring me hope suddenly left me discouraged and insecure.

But we aren't meant to hide our faces from those who are struggling. We aren't meant to brush pain off with sayings that shut people down. Instead, we should welcome honesty and open up to one another. We are meant, like Jesus, to be familiar with our own pain and each other's pain.

RAISE YOUR AWARENESS TO HIM

One evening, while I was at a community worship night, the pastor gripped the microphone, and with a tremor in his voice, admitted that he had recently started taking antianxiety medication. He explained how he prayed, worshiped, and had quiet time with God each morning, but still his mind would worry—which would then cause him to *further* worry about his worry because he knew he was supposed to worry for nothing as commanded in Philippians 4:6.

Never in my life had I heard another Christian, let alone a pastor, admit that their brain spun like my brain. If anything, I'd only heard pastors and those in Christian leadership hint that those who struggled with mental illness were not Christlike or strong enough in faith.

While the pastor explained his reasoning for getting on medication, he brought up Steve, a man in our church who was paralyzed and had to use a wheelchair. The pastor compared his brain to Steve's legs and said that sometimes our brains don't work the way they were designed to, just like the rest of our bodies at times.

Although Steve could not walk, we would never take his wheelchair from him, call him sinful, or tell him to crawl toward what God had called him to do; yet when people take anxiety medication, they are often disparaged for their lack of faith. The pastor explained that medication was his wheelchair so he could continue to run the race God had for him. Just as broken legs can take someone out of a race, a broken brain can too.

Because of that pastor's testimony, I went to the doctor the next day and was prescribed antianxiety medication. It took only two days for me to notice that my thoughts were more orderly than they'd been for as long as I could remember. I could tell the difference in the way I was thinking before and after. I could also tell when my line of thinking was becoming irrational or riddled with anxiety. More quickly, I could realign my mind. The intrusive thoughts that were like a storm in my brain and body were calmed. The waves were tamed by a small pill I had denied myself because I thought taking medication meant I did not have a strong relationship with God.

For so long, I'd wanted to read my Bible but felt crippled when I went to pick it up. If I was able to open it, I would barely understand what I read afterward because I was fighting against my brain. But with that pill, I became more motivated and focused on reading my Bible. And as I filled my mind with the Word of God, those words began to fight against the lies in my brain.

I don't have some big theological opinion about anti-anxiety medication, but I do think talking about our human experience—just like the pastor chose to do—could save a life. The pastor opening up that evening reminded me that I don't want to seek "wholeness" to present to the world. I want to seek God to give people hope when they don't have any.

After about a year of taking the medication, I weaned off it. The disciplines I'd established in Scripture stayed, but I genuinely am not sure if I would have been able to establish them without medication. That medication made it so I could better organize, place, and displace my feelings of doom enough to manage my anxiety. Even more, thoughts of ending my life were no longer such a large part of my consciousness.

Now I am still in therapy and finding a lot of peace with not being so aware of myself—because for me, too much awareness of myself has resulted in more anxiety. I believe this is because when we obsess over becoming more aware of ourselves, we become less aware of God. I've noticed that when I fixate on all I may be doing wrong and what I could be doing better, I tend to lose sight of God. The more I compare and wonder if I am measuring up, the less I experience the magnitude of his goodness.

CLAIM YOUR INHERITANCE

My thought pattern used to tell me that I was going to hurt others the way I had been hurt. There was something detrimentally wrong with me, and no matter what, I assumed I would inevitably become like my abusers.

But here's the thing. When we embrace that God is our true Father, we begin to see that we are not merely reflections of the ones who created us on earth. Rather, we are reflections of him. When we are aware of God as our Father, we become aware that we no longer receive the inheritances of the people who simply gave us our genetics and name. We actually have an inheritance in God, our Father, who makes us reflections of him. Scripture says he even makes us new and gives us new names.[3] When we are aware of him, we do not have to be so meticulously aware of ourselves, putting all the burden of change and healing on our own understanding and personal work. When we are aware of him, we start to see who he is, who we are through him, and how he heals us.

Might I invite you to pray a simple prayer? *Father, I belong to you.*[4]

May these words remind you of the inheritance available to you, of the gift you hold—and may this good news carry you even when bad memories and intrusive thoughts want to steal what you have. They cannot. And remember that all this—mental health struggles, sad thoughts, anxiety—does not make us crazy. It simply makes us human.

GOD HAS A PLAN FOR YOU

In 2023 I hosted my first conference, the Loved Already Conference. Hundreds of women showed up, and many in attendance were Christian trauma survivors. During one of the sessions, all the speakers took the stage to do a question-and-answer session. We opened the floor for the audience to take the microphone and ask anything. One of the first questions was from a young woman asking how she could stop her spiraling thoughts and suicidal ideation.

I could tell the larger audience was shocked she mentioned suicide, but they were even more shocked when I admitted from the stage that I shared the same struggles. I did this because I wanted anyone who had similar thoughts to know what I want you to know: Your faith isn't broken, and your relationship with God is not defective.

In 1 and 2 Kings there was a mighty prophet named Elijah. He lived during a very turbulent time when King Ahab had

> Your faith isn't broken, and your relationship with God is not defective.

turned away from the Lord. Ahab formed an alliance with Sidon by marrying their princess, Jezebel, and worshipping their god, Baal. Elijah was sent to show Israel the evil of their ways and encourage them to return to the Lord.

Elijah's faith was truly incredible. At his word, kings trembled, rains stopped, a jug of oil never ran dry, a boy was raised from the dead, fire fell from the sky, revival broke out, and hundreds of idolatrous prophets of Baal were executed.

But in the middle of these miraculous acts, Elijah wanted to die.

I think it's important that we look at the surrounding events to see that, though Elijah wanted God to take his life, he didn't lack genuine faithfulness.

First Kings 18:30 says Elijah "repaired the altar of the Lord, which had been torn down." We see that Elijah worked to build what was of God.

Then in verse 36, Elijah prayed, "Lord, the God of Abraham, Isaac and Israel, let it be known today that you are God in Israel and that I am your servant and have done all these things at your command." We see that Elijah knew his identity was rooted in God. In verse 40 those who worshiped Baal were seized under Elijah's leadership, and we see that Elijah had authority. In verse 46 the power of the Lord came on Elijah to the point where he outran a chariot to do what he felt God was telling him to do. We see that Elijah had the power of the Lord within him.

It is clear that Elijah showed himself very faithful.

Then, in chapter 19, Jezebel sent Elijah a threatening

message, and verses 3 and 4 explain how he became afraid, ran for his life, and "went on a day's journey into the wildness. He came to a broom bush, sat down under it and prayed that he might die." He said, "Take my life" and then he fell asleep.

Angels came to him twice, giving him bread and water, and Scripture says:

> There he came to a cave and lodged in it. And behold, the word of the Lord came to him, and he said to him, "What are you doing here, Elijah?" He said, "I have been very jealous for the Lord, the God of hosts. For the people of Israel have forsaken your covenant, thrown down your altars, and killed your prophets with the sword, and I, even I only, am left, and they seek my life, to take it away." And he said, "Go out and stand on the mount before the Lord." And behold, the Lord passed by, and a great and strong wind tore the mountains and broke in pieces the rocks before the Lord, but the Lord was not in the wind. And after the wind an earthquake, but the Lord was not in the earthquake. And after the earthquake a fire, but the Lord was not in the fire. And after the fire the sound of a low whisper. And when Elijah heard it, he wrapped his face in his cloak and went out and stood at the entrance of the cave. And behold, there came a voice to him and said, "What are you doing here, Elijah?"[5]

By gently asking Elijah the question "What are you doing here?" God prompted Elijah to remember who he was, what he was made for, and why he was on earth. And despite Elijah's turmoil, he heard God. One might think suicidal ideation is because of a lack of faith, but in Elijah's life that wasn't the case. Instead, he proves that struggles in mental health do not equate to a broken faith.

I have written in journals since I was thirteen. Recently, I looked back at some journals from college, and every day I wrote about thoughts of suicide. In college, I was the healthiest I'd ever been and my life was structured, yet anxiety ran rampant between my ears. Now my life is far less organized, and I am only averagely healthy, but a point came, finally, when I raised the question to myself, *What are you doing here?* And through that question I've slowly begun to see and believe I am here for a God-given purpose, as you are.

For the past couple of years, my suicidal thoughts have decreased drastically. I went from struggling with suicidal ideation every day to dealing with it barely at all, and now, when the thoughts do come, I can quickly combat them. I now call out the Enemy and his lies and speak the truth over myself. Scripture literally says the Enemy comes "to steal and kill and destroy."[6] Though it has taken much practice, when I begin to see the destruction of the Enemy, I rebuke it. I uninvite it. I don't declare that my faith is broken, but instead, I declare that despite my brokenness and faults, God has given me an important purpose for his kingdom, and I will not let the Enemy destroy it. Can I urge you to believe that God has given you an important purpose for his kingdom and he wants to see you complete it?

Another practice that helps me is thinking of you. I know

that might sound silly, but I mean it. I think of you. And I thought it would be fair for me to ask you, in exchange, to consider thinking about me when you are struggling with these thoughts too. Now, hear me out. Likely, if I told you I wanted to die, you would tell me that God has a plan for my life. You'd tell me I have so much to offer this world and that I should hold on to hope. You'd tell me that God did a good job making me, that so many people would be grieved if I was gone. And maybe, just maybe, you'd tell me that there is a small piece of me that someone else still needs—a piece that would inspire them to be brave and keep holding on. You'd ask me to please stick around. You'd ask me to stay.

I started this practice when I realized that I have the gift to speak truth over a lot of people through speaking, teaching, and writing—yet I was believing the truth with all my heart for other people without believing it for myself. So I ask you, What you believe for me, can you believe for yourself?

God has a plan for your life. You have so much to offer this world. God did a good job making you, and so many people would be grieved if you were gone. And not maybe, but *absolutely*, there is a piece of you that someone else needs—a piece that will inspire them to be brave and keep holding on. Would you please stick around? Would you please stay?

LIE 9

YOU'RE A BABY CHRISTIAN, SO YOUR FAITH IS IMMATURE

AT THE AGE OF SEVENTEEN, DURING MY EARLY DAYS OF walking alongside Jesus, my faith felt pure and simple. I'd call it childlike. When my high school track coach asked me how I felt about him individually coaching my biggest competition from a rival school, I said, "God will glorify himself however he wants through whoever he wants, and it doesn't have to be me." I imagine God giggling at me as I learned along the way that winning doesn't necessarily mean God's glory. But I wasn't worried about much of anything because I believed in my heart of hearts that if God is for you, no one can stand against you—and not just in a competitive sense. I believed without a shadow of a doubt God would not withhold any good thing from me.

In college, when I lacked financial support from my parents, I'd think, *I am God's girl. He always provides for his children.* I also know that financial status or surplus is not a sign of God's faithfulness (especially because I did not have it)—but the point of the matter is, my thoughts about God were simple. In many ways.

I did not read my Bible much, but I did joyfully read short devotions every day and could not wait for my morning prayer time with God. I would grab my devotional and journal like a giddy teen girl going on her first date. Through many of those short devotionals, I was encouraged and occasionally convicted. No matter how I felt about the reading, I'd post my daily devotion online hoping someone else would find hope there.

Then, a few years later, I began going to a church where people expressed judgment about how I communicated my faith. They said I "spoke about God too much" because I was a "young Christian." They said I shared my testimony too often, and sometimes they even called me a "baby Christian." Though their words were discouraging to me, I eventually went to them hoping to broach the topic with humility. Wanting to know how I might grow in my relationship with God, I asked if there was anything that pointed to me being "immature in faith" or a "baby Christian." But they said it was simply because I had not grown up in the church or known God for long enough. Their words rocked me because I did not want to appear young or immature in my faith, but even more, I didn't want to have an immature relationship with God.

After hearing the voices say enough times that devotions were "weak food for baby Christians" and not the daily bread God intended, I felt insecure. So I stopped reading devotions and praying. Even my Bible seemed like it wasn't "right" or "good enough" because it was a devotional Bible. I understand now that many devotions can be shallow, but to hear those words at that time—especially from people I looked up to in leadership who had been in the church for longer than I had been alive—made me feel so ashamed of my relationship with God.

However, those same voices did compel me to understand how to read the Bible in its context (more so out of fear than faithfulness, but nonetheless). Pretty soon after that, while at a garage sale, I found a brand-new, not-yet-used Bible that had footnotes with historical context. I also started to read Christian nonfiction books to help me understand more about God and theology. My mind and heart did seem to expand. I learned a lot about God in that short time—more than I ever had since I'd come to Christ. But the little girl in me who once ran to her Father unhindered now shrank back under the criticism, and I started to feel bogged down by the pressure to accumulate more knowledge about God.

Somewhere along the way, my relationship with God became burdensome to me. It was no longer an innocent Father-daughter relationship I treasured, but a place where I could never do, be, or know enough. My relationship with God had been the one relationship I felt I did not have to perform in—the one with my Abba. But a year later, I could have won an

Oscar for acting in that relationship. I was performing for God and his people to approve of me. I read Scripture, not to know God more, but simply because I felt pressured to learn more from a scholarly perspective and become a "mature enough Christian." I memorized Bible verses, not to apply them to my life and remember who God was, but to avoid appearing dumb in front of others when talking about the Bible.

My trauma and obsession with how authority figures thought of me took hold of my relationship with God. Going to God in prayer now felt complicated because I questioned if I was doing it wrong. I didn't want to face him in my "immaturity." What used to bring me peace suddenly shook me with fear. I had lost my childlike faith.

CHILDLIKENESS BREEDS COMPASSION, NOT CRITICS

Three out of four Sundays, my church does an altar call by inviting people to have a relationship with Jesus Christ and commit their lives to him. Three out of four altar calls, the pastor asks us to put our heads down and close our eyes before he asks the people who want to dedicate their lives to Christ to raise their hands. Every time, I cannot resist keeping at least one eye open and looking left to right. It is such a great joy to me to see other people beginning a relationship in which I have found so much healing and fulfillment.

Sometimes, the same people who dedicated their lives and

raised their hands in prior weeks will raise their hands again. While I have heard others criticize such people, each time I see someone's hand go up, tears fill my eyes no matter how many times I have seen that hand go up in the past. I know they are trying their best to draw close to the heart of God, and I think their actions—no matter how others perceive them—are vulnerable.

I, too, believe God is more pleased with someone who raises a hand repeatedly than someone who doesn't ever give God and faith a try. I think God looks upon those of us who are trying with compassion and tear-filled eyes, not criticism.

While in college, I had a friend and teammate named Alexia. She was a star pole-vaulter and a popular sorority girl, and lots of boys crushed over her. From the outside looking in, one would think she was perfect. To be honest, I thought so too until I found out she'd grown up with an alcoholic father. And just a few months after we connected over our broken homes and wounded hearts, her father died while attempting sobriety on his own.

One afternoon while I was studying in a common area, Alexia walked past crying. I don't remember the ins and outs of our conversation, but I do remember her sobbing and pouring her heart out to me while trying to catch her breath. We were both sitting in high-top chairs as she cried, and I listened for only a short time before I looked at her and said what had once been said to me: "Alexia, you just need to trust God."

She wailed so loud after I said these words I pulled away in shock. Students began to walk out of their classrooms, and

Alexia screamed, "Tori, my dad died!" She then fell into me. I wrapped my arms around her and carried her to a couch lower to the ground. Once we were stable, I held her in my lap and rocked her like a baby until her crying subsided.

Tears rolled from my eyes—half-heartedly for Alexia but also because I regretted what I'd said. I had thought it was the best response to give, but I had inadvertently criticized my friend's faith when I should have led with compassion. I was trying to sound like a mature Christian, but I lost my childlikeness in the process—which led me to lose compassion as my reflex. I think this happened because I was no longer looking to God. I was looking to imitate those who looked religiously intelligent.

In Jesus' day, the religiously intelligent people were the Pharisees. They distinguished themselves by being critical, like on the Sabbath day when Jesus was compassionately healing the sick. That day with Alexia, I learned that what may sound accurate theologically is not always best for pastoring or shepherding, which means guiding people to a safe place, kindly and lovingly.

With Alexia, I said no more words because I realized the words I had used were not the right ones. I wish I would have answered her differently, but I said what the Christians I followed had taught me to say. Jesus, who was filled with compassion when he looked upon people, didn't cross my mind in that moment.

Sometimes we try to mend broken hearts with words that work as well as school glue on grandma's broken china. The glue just makes the beautiful pieces sticky, and the dishes are bound to break again. Similarly, our unthoughtful maxims can cause more harm than good. Now, I am utterly convinced that God will have vast mercy on those of us who didn't articulate the theology right every time—but I do believe he will be deeply concerned with whether we chose mercy, showed compassion, and loved other people.

A SAFE PLACE FOR THE CHILDLIKE

It is important to be considerate with our words when we are around people who are new to faith. Thoughtful words make us a safe place. We must not only *mean* well but also *do* well with our words. After all, death and life, and nothing in between, are in the power of the tongue.[1] Also, silence is a perfectly sound response. Or "What you are going through sounds so hard." A hug given. Cookies or a meal sent. Be a safe place, and then point people toward their Forever Safest Place with encouraging words and a reflection of Christlike love.

If there's anything I've learned from being so broken and loved—and from loving the broken—it's that we need a lot less advice and a lot more listeners. We need fewer people pointing fingers and more people holding hands. We don't always need to fix people. People are not projects. We need to simply *be with* people.

The church should never become a place where church members—meant to be family—define us as inadequate and ill-equipped in our faith. Faith isn't something we conjure. Faith is a gift given by God. When we give people grief for not having enough faith or not being mature enough in the faith, it can take people further and further from God. Jesus was the man who looked upon crowds and had compassion upon them.[2] This kind of empathy and understanding is not a New Age idea. It is a characteristic of Jesus.

Might we remember the Beatitudes when we are met with empty platitudes and shallow solutions?

> Blessed are the poor in spirit,
>> for theirs is the kingdom of heaven.
> Blessed are those who mourn,
>> for they will be comforted.
> Blessed are the meek,
>> for they will inherit the earth.
> Blessed are those who hunger and thirst for
>> righteousness,
>> for they will be filled.
> Blessed are the merciful,
>> for they will be shown mercy.
> Blessed are the pure in heart,
>> for they will see God.
> Blessed are the peacemakers,
>> for they will be called children of God.
> Blessed are those who are persecuted because of
>> righteousness,
>> for theirs is the kingdom of heaven.

Blessed are you when people insult you, persecute you and falsely say all kinds of evil against you because of me. Rejoice and be glad, because great is your reward in heaven, for in the same way they persecuted the prophets who were before you.[3]

If we put words in God's mouth about what is most holy, or if we shame individuals for their faith life within the church, we don't leave space for honest conversation. We instead become congregants in competition with one another rather than a community that brings one another closer to Christ. The church becomes exactly what the Enemy wants it to be when we belittle those for where they are in their faith or in their suffering: a place where people are unable to heal or be honest. As God's people, we should act as if we are holding welcome signs that say, You Are Safe Here.

A childlike faith grows out of safety. When I initially came to Jesus, I felt safe with God and with my community. My childlike faith withered the more unsafe I felt. The more I thought God viewed me as not smart enough, not holy enough, and not faithful enough, the more I drew back from him. Now, I don't want us to have immature theology and excuse it as childlike faith, but I also don't want us to lose the intimate relationship with God that so many miss out on when they think faith needs to be performative.

First Peter 2:1–3 gives us an image of what it looks like to remain childlike while still growing in our faith and remain compassionate as others are in different places in their faith. "Therefore, rid yourselves of all malice and all deceit, hypocrisy, envy, and slander of every kind. Like new-born babies, crave pure spiritual milk, so that by it you may grow up in your salvation, now that you have tasted that the Lord is good." Indeed, we can grow mature in our faith, but it shouldn't result in slander of those who are maybe "less mature" or whose faith is simply different from ours.

I think of Alexia and know her cries were not a measure of her faith or maturity. Her cries were a brave call for help. As a Christian, she felt safe enough in her faith to feel and cry to God. Crying out, grieving with God, sitting in our hurt, asking questions, and reading devotions are all signs that our faith is fervent—because in our childlikeness we know our God as Father. We cry out because we believe he is a present Father who answers. We cry out with a hope for his response. This is faith. He meets us right where we are, and he's safe enough to grow with. Embracing this reality is what it means to know God.

GOING BACK TO A CHILDLIKE FAITH

So what does keeping and reclaiming our childlike faith look like?

One Sunday morning during church, I felt an overwhelming awe as I reflected on my life during a time of prayer. As I've shared, I'd been through many difficult circumstances throughout my upbringing and into my adulthood, yet I felt so thankful to get to do my work despite where I came from.

However, while juggling family, a ministry, and a business, I was growing increasingly tired and impatient with my loved ones, and I didn't love who I was becoming.

I'd always wondered how some in ministry preached the Word of God, stayed close to the church body, and read his Word but also treated people so poorly. This time taught me that poor treatment of God's people comes easily when we treat ourselves poorly and neglect our time with God. During this season, my work became less of a calling and more of a means of self-harm. I was pushing myself too hard to get the work done, and I know it broke God's heart because I did it all in his name.

Genuinely, I loved my work, and I believed wholeheartedly I was working for the glory of God. But at many moments, people would *not* have known me as a disciple by my love— and that terrified me. People had cautioned me that my platform or influence could outgrow my character. I actually appreciated the caution and held tight to it because I'd witnessed ministers and leaders be given much only to become jerks. And a jerk was the opposite of what I wanted to be, so I asked God to tell me what to do.

As I sat next to my husband during the church service, I wondered if I was doing what God had called me to in exactly the way he wanted me to do it. I was indeed young.

The next week, on Sunday morning in worship, those senses were amplified—immense gratitude coupled with an apprehensive questioning of myself. Those feelings swirled through my mind. God nudged me and said, *Go to the altar.*

I stood there as the worship songs played, but my feet were cinder blocks. I didn't move. The more I felt God telling me to go up, the stiller I remained.

Typically, people went up to the altar if one of our pastors did a traditional altar call and invited people to surrender their lives to Jesus. I worried that people in my church would assume something must be wrong with me if went up to the altar on my own—and I did not want anyone to think I was depressed, struggling financially, or worse, not saved. So I stayed standing, having an argument with my own self, distracted by how disobedient I was, swaying in the four corners of my chair even though I felt a nudge to position myself at the altar, as if at the feet of Jesus.

Week after week, I'd feel the same heavy weight. You'd think going up to the altar would be simple, but I could not shake the worry of what people would think. I questioned everything: my intentions, the validity of my career, my intelligence, and my calling. I wondered if deep down I was a total jerk. And week after week, through my thankfulness and fear, awe and anxiety, God would nudge me to approach him at the altar in a position of surrender. But I couldn't walk in front of the entire congregation because I was afraid of being judged.

In this struggle, God revealed to me that I did not have a simple disobedience or rebellion problem. My reluctance to move was a reflection of my relationship with God and the work I was doing. I cared more about looking good than doing what he said when he said to. I was working and producing so others would see me as good—not so I could become truly good in the unseen moments with God.

This realization was heartbreaking; I didn't want to care about people's perspectives more than I cared about God. After all, those people aren't the ones I will be answering to in heaven. God is. So finally one morning, as God nudged me during another church service, I staved off my fear of what people thought of me as much as I could. Hoping to surrender every little piece of my life to God, I walked up to the front of the church and knelt with my hands open as hundreds of people looked my way.

My body was in the same position my heart needed to be. Low. Surrendered. Humble.

I was not holding a microphone in my hand, witnessing, proclaiming, or teaching. Instead, people saw me bent down low. A confession of disobedience. An apology for my vanity. A complete surrender of my ministry and life to God. Then peace washed over me. I felt such a deep relief.

Soon after this weight left me, a woman in the front row came and laid her hand on me. "Tori, can I give you a word?" she asked. I was the only one at the altar, and I was sure she was going to say, "You are a disobedient jerk." I was ready to accept it. I replied, "Of course."

She said, "God is so pleased with your surrender to him." Then she described an image of me walking on a path and picking up stones. As I continued to walk, I handed Jesus the stones, saying, "These are yours. I will give them to you." Then God gave them back to me, giving me permission to build and work with them. The woman said this simple act of giving back and forth was surrender. God gave her the words to reassure me when she said, "You are walking on the right path, surrendering it all. He is pleased with you." The song finished, I stood up, and then I saw about ten other people around me at the altar.

One of my pastors walked onstage and pointed out how many people had come forward without an altar call, saying he was surprised when "the first girl came up." People rarely approached the altar without a pastor's call. Normally I would have started shaking with anxiety and humiliation at someone pointing that out, but I knew in that moment that God wanted to use the situation to show me something.

My pastor and the people who may have seen me approach the altar perceived the situation through a blurry lens and may have made assumptions. But the woman who spoke to me and encouraged me represented God. And other people in the congregation took it as permission to seek God at the altar for themselves. God sees our hearts for what they are, where they are, and he loves us not for who we are supposed to be but for who we are. He calls us to him not when we arrive but while we are still searching and wandering children.

I was under constant strain from questioning whether I was the right person to do God's work. All that strain dissipated when God made it clear to me that the "right person" means anyone who has their eyes fixed on him and is willing to do what he says. He did not care about my age, intellect, or lack thereof. He cared about my concern for his opinion over everyone else's and my willingness to surrender. God isn't concerned if we are showing up to him "right." He just revels in us showing up with a childlike, surrendered heart.

REMAIN CHILDLIKE

For me, I preserve this childlikeness by reminding myself of what drew me to God when I first accepted him as mine. I remember that he isn't just a grand mystery that can't be fully understood in all his splendor. He is also my Father who wants me to maintain the wonder and joy of my salvation. I am on an adventure with God, trying to see him in the parts of my life that may seem silly to others.

To have a childlike faith is to stay curious. I will never know it all, but I continue to be amazed that I get to know God. I remain excited about my time with God, I tell people about my time with him, and I tell people about God—not to posture or come off as especially holy or scholarly but because I want people to be giddy about the God I am giddy about.

In Matthew 18, Jesus' disciples came to him with a burning question. They asked, "Who is the greatest in the kingdom of heaven?" The disciples puffed out their chests, giving reasons it should be them. I imagine Jesus, with a smirk and wink, responding to their question with an answer that tilted their heads. He instructed them to become like children and welcome children to him.

Jesus said that those who are childlike are the greatest in

the kingdom of heaven.[4] This means Jesus is safe to be child-like with, and those who turn your childlikeness away are not like Jesus. They are just confused about what it means to follow him. If you are new to Christ, you are not immature. You are not less of a Christian because you've known God for fewer years than someone else. Actually, our childlikeness is exactly what God is looking for.

> Our childlikeness is exactly what God is looking for.

In 2 Kings 5 a man named Naaman is described as a valiant soldier who happened to have leprosy. Naaman's wife was served by an unnamed slave girl. When the young girl saw Naaman's leprosy, she said, "If only my master would see the prophet who is in Samaria! He would cure him of his leprosy." This young girl who was enslaved had a faith bold and child-like enough to speak into the problems of her masters.

Naaman, in turn, went to a prophet named Elisha, who instructed him to dip his body in the Jordan seven times for his flesh to be cleaned. This story makes me think about the time God asked me to go to the altar, because when Naaman heard the instruction, he was upset like me. Naaman thought Elisha would simply call upon the name of the Lord and wave his hand over his body for the leprosy to be healed.

Although Naaman was enraged, his servants encouraged him through their childlike, humble faith when they said, "My father, if the prophet had told you to do some great thing, would you not have done it?" So Naaman, inspired by their example, became childlike himself. He did not do anything grand to be healed, but rather, physically lowered himself into the water seven times.

Scripture then says that his body was restored like a child's.[5] Naaman's childlike humility healed his illness. How much more might our childlike faith heal us?

God wants you as his child, even as someone who is still growing in your faith. If you ask questions, if you have doubts, or if you worry, his Word will guide you back to himself, not push you away. I imagine one of the reasons God appreciates a childlike faith is because it gives him room to work. When we have pride—thinking we know so much or have come to a completion in our faith—there is not much space for God to speak into.

So I'm going back to a childlike faith—a faith that is willing to lower myself wherever God asks, a faith that is giddy for God, regardless of my inadequacies or lack of knowledge. I have now known and walked with Jesus for ten years, and though that is significantly less than many, I understand that time is relative to God. What's more, God measures our faith in his own way.

YOU CAN'T CHANGE YOUR STORY

WHEN I EMANCIPATED FROM THE FOSTER-CARE SYSTEM, I was instantly homeless, as 20 percent of youth who age out become.[1] However, a woman named Tonya who was a mentor and minister to me in my junior high years allowed me to live with her. Later, my track coach, Scott, welcomed me into his family, and I moved in with him. To this day, Tonya is like a mom to me, so I refer to her as a mother figure in my life (but not as my mom because I do still have a relationship with my mom). I also refer to Scott as my dad.

I moved in with Scott when I was eighteen, weeks after I graduated high school. To say we butted heads a lot would be an understatement. One of the reasons we fought often was because he wanted to spend time with me, but I didn't have the same value. He expressed that we didn't have the years that biological parents and children would've naturally had together, so he wanted to spend time with me the summer before I went off to college. But instead, I'd run off, go clubbin', spend the night at friends' houses, and do anything except spend time with Scott. Truth be told, I wasn't ready to be that close with him and make up for the years we hadn't shared while I was growing up. Instead, I wanted to make up for the fun I didn't have in my childhood.

When an argument would break out, I would usually finish it by screaming, "You're kicking me out! Fine! I'm leaving!" And then slam the door behind me. Scott would open the door and say the same thing every time: "This home will always be your home. This room will always be your room. I'll be your dad no matter what and whenever you decide to come back." I'd leave for hours on end, determined not to return, until I realized he'd never kicked me out at all. The narrative I was functioning from was a lie. Eventually, after so many times of Scott *not* kicking me out, I started to believe him and stopped the antics.

Despite being taken in and adopted by my track coach and having a mother figure who I spoke with regularly, I convinced myself and others during my young adulthood that I did not have a family to lean on. I don't know why I did this, but I imagine it's because I wanted the love, the nurturing, and the kind of mom I didn't have. Whatever the reason was, I see now that past narratives can be hard to escape, even when they are no longer true.

This story—that I no longer had a family—led to self-pity

and compelled people to pity me. For example, when people saw the dysfunctional relationship I had with Kimberly, they assumed I was just innocently wanting a mother figure in my life. While that was accurate, the narrative also tried to excuse my destructive patterns of returning to toxic relationships without acknowledging their unhealthiness. The truth was, I *did* have a family. I had multiple families who loved me radically, but I kept telling this story because it was the one I'd known for years. This story had become my identity in a sense, and when good people like Scott and Tonya came into my life, I didn't even notice I was telling a story that was no longer true.

In psychology this way of referring to and functioning from stories that are no longer true is called *cognitive dissonance*, and it occurs when we live or think in ways that contradict one another.[2] Sometimes we sabotage situations because when life becomes too stable, we yearn for chaos since it is what we are used to and comfortable in. We want chaos because we know how to navigate it better than stability. Yet it's important to tell the story as it is, or else we could be taking the pen from God and missing out altogether on the good story he is writing.

TELL THE TRUE STORY

One Christmas, my husband, Jacob, and I were organizing presents, figuring out what to give who. Christmas was a lot of work at the time with his four siblings' families and their children. Then we had to think about my families, which included at least my biological mom and sister, my adoptive dad and adoptive sisters, and Tonya's family. Sometimes we'd throw a foster family in there who wanted to get together for a bit during the break. And of course, church family, neighbors, friends, and some others. We had many gifts to sort and give.

One of the highest-quality items in the mix of gifts was a leather bag. As we were figuring out who to give it to, I of course suggested Kimberly. Then I threw it on her pile, which included many of the other best presents we were gifting that year. Jacob paused organizing, looked around, and said, "You've already gotten her so much, and you never give your family any of the best stuff. Let's give this to Tonya. That's something she would never buy for herself, but I bet she would use every day." He proceeded to toss the bag from Kimberly's pile to my *actual* mother figure's pile.

I was taken aback by his comment. I thought, *Of course I get my family nice stuff. I love my family and want them to have nice things from me.* But when I looked around at how I'd divided up the presents, I saw that my families' presents were far less than Kimberly's. When Jacob tossed the bag from one pile to the other, I realized my perception was blurred. By then, Tonya had been my *actual* mother figure for nearly a decade.

In my relationship with Kimberly, I would get her flowers and gifts, make ample time for her, and pick up the hobbies she was interested in. At the same time, I had neglected Tonya, who had poured into me since my junior high years.

The little girl in me—the child who would do anything for others to love her—broke a little more that day, and I needed to sit in that brokenness. It was through the cracks of my brokenness that light shined through, and I became more aware that the story I once lived was no longer the story I was now living.

I did give Tonya the leather bag for Christmas. As frugal and modest as she is, she never would have bought herself such a treat—but she's used it every day for years now, just as Jacob said.

> It was through the cracks of my brokenness that light shined through, and I became more aware that the story I once lived was no longer the story I was now living.

That experience revealed that I was telling myself a story that was not true. Despite all the other love I already had, I thought gaining the love of others would make me most lovable. It was evident in the gifts I gave and hours I spent. Maybe we could call that epiphany a Christmas miracle.

When I rediscovered the old truth that I was loved by many, I felt a bit like the Prodigal Daughter. I'd forgotten I had a flourishing relationship with Tonya and had thrown all my pearls and leather bags before Kimberly. Tonya had even stood in as my mom at my wedding. She answered her phone for me on countless late nights, which always brought peace to my hurting heart. She used to be my best friend, and when I finally recognized she'd never left and I turned my heart back toward her, there she was, waiting, like the father of the Prodigal Son, for me to come home. She understood every bit of why I left and why I squandered her kindness and sacrifices.

I hate admitting it, but the truth is, I'd focused so much on people's lack of affection for me that I completely lost sight of the love and care people *did* have for me. And I'd done the same with God's love.

There will always be people who don't love us the way we imagined or hoped they would. But if we fixate on the lack, we can neglect our good stories. When we focus on the world's lack of love for us rather than God's abundant love for us, we can become blind to love altogether.

While I do believe we are supposed to love those who do not love us or treat us the way we want to be treated, I don't think we are supposed to do so at the expense of those who are lavishing us with love and wanting to be in our lives. I also do not believe we are supposed to attach ourselves to people in ways where we miss out on the good relationships we already have.

After this Christmas miracle, I opened myself up to my family more than I ever had. I started sending flowers to Tonya instead of Kimberly. Rather than giving gifts to those I *wanted* to love me, I gave to my family—those who had never left and always loved me. The time I'd once offered to others, hoping to prove I was lovable, I began to spend with people who deemed me loved already. I can now say I am closer to my adoptive families than ever before.

It's worth asking ourselves how the stories in our lives

have changed so we don't function out of narratives that are no longer true. The facts of my past were still the same. I, the narrator, simply changed my perspective, so my perspective of myself began to shift significantly too. I went from believing I wasn't loved and wanted to knowing I was, indeed, loved and wanted.

Maybe you don't have people, or maybe you have not fully accepted the people who have accepted you. May we embrace what we have rather than grieving what we don't. May we see the story that is true and embrace the love we have been given.

ATTACH SECURELY

Another person I had all along was my friend Maddie. We remained friends after college and even moved to the same region of the country. When I was experiencing the turmoil of other relationships, Maddie bluntly told me that our friendship was overwhelming her. She was steadily being there for me and carrying a lot of my heartache. Thankfully, when she told me this, she assured me she was not going to leave me, but she kindly communicated that the drama in my life had become too much to bear. Her soft ability to tell me the truth and the years of trust between us made me take a good, hard look at myself.

Because I am a foster mom, the topic of attachment styles often comes up in the regular foster-care trainings we are required to take. While I don't find many foster-care trainings too exciting, I find the subject of attachment styles to be riveting, and I think you will too.

Get this. There are four different attachment styles that people develop as children: secure, avoidant, anxious, and disorganized.[3] People with codependent tendencies, like myself, tend to have an anxious attachment style. When forming relationships, those with anxious attachment styles are usually clingy and highly sensitive to criticism. They also struggle to be alone, seek approval from others, and have significant fears of abandonment.

Because I've lived through all these things, I have learned these behaviors are quick ways to corrode relationships.

Sometimes relationships end because they need to—because seasons, people, and circumstances change. For a time in my life, however, my relationships were ending because of me. When we are dependent on people, we lack self-sufficiency, independence, and dependency on God, which can cause us to place this burden upon others, which in turn causes us to burn through relationships.

Now, generally speaking, society recognizes the trauma response of a person distancing themselves and not trusting others. But a lesser-understood trauma response is latching on to others and trusting them too quickly and too much. In my relationships, I was terrified of feeling abandoned again, so I would latch on and grip people until I squeezed so hard they wanted to get away. I also often "trauma dumped," meaning I continually told people about the traumatic events in my life and sought their validation and comfort without considering their feelings. I had very high expectations for my relationships, hoping to receive affirmation as if it could be given to me limitlessly.

To stop wrecking relationships, I've had to confess that I am not limitless and neither are other people. Only God is limitless. We can't burn through God, which is why we must fully depend on him. While friendships can be therapeutic, they cannot be therapy. While relationships can be healing, they cannot be our sole healer.

> While friendships can be therapeutic, they cannot be therapy. While relationships can be healing, they cannot be our sole healer.

Instead of expecting so much from one or two friends, I've found a lot more security and stability in wrapping myself in a community of people who have many different gifts. I want to move toward not overusing people who are generous enough to hold space for me.

Maybe you're like me and you care genuinely about your relationships and the people in your life. You want to give and love well, but you are struggling to see the fine line between being a loving friend and being an overbearing one. I get it. But if we take some steps back—which can be a scary experience, I know—perhaps we will get the time and space we need to observe our own actions and patterns.

In the past few years I've seen many books and heard many ideas about forming healthy boundaries, mainly for the purpose of controlling what others do. For example, we do not allow someone to contact us if they continually hurt us. We do not invite people over for the holidays if they get drunk and lash out at loved ones. These are great standards, but I'm finding I need to make fewer boundaries for others and more for myself. You've heard it before, and it is true: We can only control ourselves. This is a good place to focus when our relationships seem out of control.

Maybe instead of going to a friend's house a few times a week, we should go a few times a month. Maybe instead of telling people our deepest, darkest secrets within the first few times hanging out, we should listen well and be vulnerable with discernment. When we know we are fully known and fully loved by God, this becomes much easier because we aren't seeking to be fully known and loved by anyone else. We aren't seeking an attachment we've never had because we are fully known and securely attached to him.

BOUNDARIES ARE LOVING TOO

Setting boundaries for ourselves is not about shutting ourselves off from others but rather giving people room to breathe. This isn't an act of loving people less but creating space to love like Christ more. When we aren't constantly with people, serving them and showing up for them, we have space to show up and spend time with God. We give them, in turn, room to serve God too. When we ask for too much of someone's time and energy, we take them away from the other places they are meant to serve.

On the other hand, when we have healthy relationships, we free up space for others to make other friends and form a vast community of support. While all of this might sound obvious, it took me a while to learn it. I even used labels to normalize my tendencies—naming people my "best friends" and claiming we were "always there for one another"—when in reality I was latching on to people in unhealthy ways and fearing I would lose them. In these and other ways, I have been overbearing in the lives of others.

Here's another problem we face when we are inordinately afraid of losing people: The fear can make us more tolerant of toxicity, abuse, and other unhealthy behaviors in relationships. Unhealthy relationships perpetuate our issues of codependency. I used to tolerate a lot because I didn't want to lose people. Now I establish boundaries because I don't want to lose people. I establish boundaries because I do not want to lose myself.

If you don't understand what I am saying, I don't blame you. Seeing these patterns within ourselves can be difficult, so I want to explain this clearly: When we have codependent tendencies, we fall into a cycle of dysfunctional relationships. First, we lose who we are through the trauma we experience in the unhealthy relationship. Then, as we try to be who the other person wants us to be, we grow weary. We seek their approval, and when we do not receive it, we try even harder to gain their love and acceptance. Our efforts are not malicious; they are merely attempts to survive and keep the relationship. But eventually we fall short or explode or fail, so our efforts don't actually maintain the relationship. They break it. After the relationship falls apart, we apologize for the relationship's rupture and start trying yet again to be who the other person wants us to be to avoid losing them.

But if we form healthy boundaries for ourselves, we won't fall into this pattern, and we won't lose ourselves.

Maddie is a friend I felt safe with because she had been around for so long. When we invest in relationships like these, our anxious attachment styles start to fade away. We learn to maintain stable relationships. And we learn to receive criticism from those who love us without being crushed. When we are surrounded by a community, we experience good friends who do not simply call us out of our unhealthy ways. They call us up into a love that is secure.

YOU CAN CHANGE YOUR STORY

As I write this, I have the healthiest relationships and friendships I've ever had. Relationships will always take work and friendships will have rifts, but lowering my expectations of people and believing their best intentions has helped me not get down when they don't meet the expectations that I might hope for. I used to always be the friend who reached out to make plans. Now I will typically initiate a get-together, and after that hangout time is over, I will wait for the other person in the relationship to initiate our next outing. I believe we were created to live in community with each other; however, if I sense a friend wants space, I will simply give space.

I also attribute having better relationships to knowing my identity more. I used to believe the responses of others defined me, but now I know that only God defines me.

When people's love comes and goes, God's love remains steady and secure. God does not become annoyed or overwhelmed with our clinginess and smothering. God cannot be smothered. So as much as you want to run to people, run to him. Trauma dump through your prayers. Cry in your worship. Scream in his face. Bang on his chest. Get too attached to him. God is big enough to handle us, and he will not see you as a burden. He will hold you as his child. He will listen like a friend. He will not leave, and when we experience his never-abandoning love, we feel free to let our dependency on people transform to dependence on God. This is how we keep our people and how we keep ourselves, because God does not just save us. He keeps us.

YOU HAVE TO FIGURE OUT YOUR CALLING

I HAD COMPLETELY LOST MYSELF. KNEADING. MIXING. Squishing. Stirring. Shaping. Proofing. Baking. *Ding*.

Right after the bread came out of the oven, I proudly snapped a picture and sent it to Kimberly, who inspired me to make bread because she'd taken it on as a hobby. It's as if the oven alarm went off and woke me up to the fact that I'd picked up several hobbies because Kimberly approved of them—but I didn't know which ones were my own.

Track and field actually was my choice. After being isolated in foster care and labeled negatively by many, track became the glue that connected me with others. People saw me how I wanted to be seen because of track—talented, accomplished, the good kid. Track also helped me form some of the strongest relationships in my life, most significantly with my high school coach who became my adoptive dad. Track taught me that hobbies and the performance of them could lead to the relationships I desired.

I sat at my kitchen table staring at two hot loaves. Then my face fell into my hands, and tears slid between my fingers. I desperately wanted to be wanted, so much so that I'd learned whatever necessary to connect. But with these two loaves of bread, I could see how much of myself I did not know. I likely would have never pursued this hobby on my own.

I had come to the point where I had no idea what I liked or didn't like. And while making bread is a small matter that has very little to do with who God has made me to be, this example helped me see I didn't even know what I was good at. I didn't know my calling, I didn't know what God wanted of me, and I didn't know myself.

The jobs I'd taken on, the hobbies, the friends, everything that surrounded me—my life was driven not only by wanting to be accepted, but also by whatever seemed to draw me closer to others. Other people's dreams and aspirations became my own, putting me into roles where I didn't belong.

Of course, God created us for connection. Relationships are good. But how much of our lives do we spend doing what others want us to do rather than exploring what God might want of us?

On top of this, the voices I heard seemed to be obsessed with "calling." If I expressed any kind of interest or idea about what I aspired to do, the typical response was, "You need to make sure you are called to that." So the impending doom of not hearing the audible voice of God or seeing a sign falling out of the sky made me hesitant to do much of anything other than what those around me deemed most acceptable. I was hesitant to even try something because I didn't know if it was my calling.

Since high school, I'd been given opportunities to speak and share my testimony, but being called to anything that would take me away from my baby felt sinful in the culture and community we lived in. Being a mom was never the wrong answer, so I embraced motherhood.

For the first year and a half of my son's life he slept often and on a schedule. I know this is not relatable to many moms, but I found the newborn stage very easy with my firstborn, and I felt like God was granting me the space each day to do something outside of motherhood as well. It was important to me that whatever I did, I could remain at home and have it revolve around my husband—again, because that was what I understood to be a "holy" choice. This is one of the many factors that led me to write my first book, *Fostered*. I could write whenever I had time. My husband could still work wherever and whenever he had the opportunity to work. And when my son fell asleep, I'd write.

Though it felt like such a long time, I soon received a book deal that led to more opportunities to speak. I always felt obligated to receive Jacob's approval, but he never hesitated to say, "You have to do it." Yet women in the church suggested my work was making my husband sad. Because he was not receiving opportunities that appeared as "big" as mine, surely my work was demeaning to my husband's identity. The narrative I couldn't escape again and again was that I was the problem.

I look back and believe these opportunities were God-led because I carried on despite caring so deeply about what others said about me. I continued to pursue and accept opportunities to speak and write. When I traveled for speaking engagements, I'd choose the flight that got me there and back with the least amount of time away from my children. Usually I'd wake up at three thirty in the morning to drive to the airport, speak in the morning or early afternoon, and return the same day. Then I usually wrote when the kids went to bed at night. I'd lay the kids down at eight and stay at my laptop writing until two the next morning.

In between words I'd wrestle with what it meant to be a good Christian woman, but stories spilled out of me. Those stories were like prayers that allowed me to see who God is. He is our Father who always stays. He is our safe place who holds us when no one else will. He is our Creator who accepts us right where we are. Over time, I didn't meet the churchy Christian woman standards anymore, but I did meet with God. And over time, through my writing and ministry, I learned that God is much less concerned with calling us toward a vocation and much more concerned with calling us toward him.

> God is much less concerned with calling us toward a vocation and much more concerned with calling us toward him.

YOU ARE A WITNESS

The more I shared my story, the more I witnessed that the worst parts of life could be made good. And the more I shared my story, the more I wanted to be in God's Word and worship him because I had to reflect on and testify to what he had done in my life.

The more I explored the facets of what God called me to, the more I understood that my vocation is not writing. My vocation is not teaching or preaching. My vocation is not motherhood or wifehood. My vocation is love. My vocation is to be a witness of God's love. And the answer was never within me. I've realized that the answer to finding myself and my calling was *never* within me. The way to know ourselves is through God.

In Scripture the word *witness* is most commonly used to refer to people who have experienced something and openly testified to it.[1] A *witness* is a person who guaranteed, or swore to, the truth of something. As followers of God, we are called to be witnesses—which I think clears up the question of what we are meant to do. Now, I don't need for my life to demonstrate my gift in writing or my talent in speaking or my ability to make a home. I want my life and my witness to point to the truth of God's love. Nothing more and nothing less.

I was angry at the way others' careless words caused me to wrestle with and overcomplicate my identity and calling. But in anger, I threw off the idea of pursuing a calling and declared

I would pursue God. It is the best decision my anger has ever led me to.

Viewing my calling not as a role or job, but as love, has continually brought me back to community and serving the poor. No matter how many books I sign or how big my stages are, I remember that Jesus said, "Truly I tell you, whatever you did for one of the least of these brothers and sisters of mine, you did for me."[2] If everything you do fails, or if your position is someday stripped away, it actually doesn't matter because your vocation remains. Jesus also said, "By this everyone will know that you are my disciples, if you love one another."[3] We won't be known by our titles. We won't be known by our opinions. We won't be known by accolades. We will be known by our love.

> We won't be known by our opinions. We won't be known by accolades. We will be known by our love.

I could share many scriptures that led me during this time in my life. The Passion Translation of the Bible became a special kind of companion to me, so I want to share this passage with you. I share it for the ones who have lost themselves and feel far from God. For the ones who feel like their calling is unaccepted by those who are supposed to cheer them on. For the ones who are seeking answers, I hope these words bring you back to Jesus. He calls you his beloved and whispers:

Arise, my dearest. Hurry, my darling.

Come away with me!

I have come as you have asked

to draw you to my heart and lead you out.

For now is the time, my beautiful one.

The season has changed,

the bondage of your barren winter has ended,

and the season of hiding is over and gone. . . .

Can you not discern this new day of destiny

breaking forth around you?

The early signs of my purposes and plans

are bursting forth. . . .

Let me see your radiant face and hear your sweet voice.

How beautiful your eyes of worship

and lovely your voice in prayer.

You must catch the troubling foxes,

those sly little foxes that hinder our relationship.

For they raid our budding vineyard of love

to ruin what I've planted within you.

Will you catch them and remove them for me?

We will do it together.[4]

This scripture stamped this season of my life, as it reminded me that God simply wants intimacy with us. During this time, I was able to detach my religious beliefs and relationship with God from what would make me most acceptable to man. I finally understood that God had already accepted me. Losing myself and finding God meant burying and having a funeral for the idea that being loved and accepted by people would satisfy. I found myself by losing what I thought I wanted most. Finding myself and finding my calling came from finding God.

YOUR CALLING IS LOVE

If you're in a place where you've built your life on the opinions of others or if you feel stuck or lost or like you just don't know who you are meant to be, rest assured, beloved. God knows you, and if you take the time to get to know him, he will show you the most dazzling version of yourself you've ever seen.

Maybe you're thinking, *Yeah. That sounds nice, but how do I actually get to know God?* Galatians 5:6 says, "The only thing that counts is faith expressing itself through love." Simply do the next thing in love. When you are living with the intention to love as Christ loved, you begin to notice him everywhere. You will find joy, and you will begin to know what your purpose in Christ is. I have questioned many things in my faith journey, but the one thing that remains consistent is that the more I attempt to love my neighbor, the more of the joy of the Lord I experience, and the more I know God and precisely what he has called me to.

You, beloved, do not have to be shrunk down to fit into a box. Your calling to love is vast. Simply follow Love.

TO LOVE MEANS TO STAY, NO MATTER WHAT

MY SIBLING, WHO I WAS SEPARATED FROM IN THE foster-care system, came to visit our family. I was twenty-four and living in Minnesota, and she was fourteen and living in Ohio near our hometown. We spent our week together eating at our favorite restaurants, learning about what we missed when we were separated, and exploring new ice cream shops, the Mall of America, and places with oversized soft pretzels. The Lord, indeed, does restore what the locusts have eaten.[1]

After the week was over, my sibling told me she was not in the safest living situation. She wanted to live with us but did not want to move schools. Unlike a lot of my peers, I'd hoped to stay in my hometown for a long time, if not for the rest of my life. Though my hometown is not big or flashy, I was disappointed when Jacob's first job out of college took us all the way to Minnesota.

At the time of my sibling's visit, my relationship with Kimberly was also in its unhealthiest state. Her threats and actions became unsafe to our family, and we were hoping to move away—but had it not been for my sibling's situation, I don't know if we would have mustered the gumption to leave.

I was unraveling the patterns of my own codependency and detaching myself from the relationship with Kimberly. Yet leaving the town that married my life to hers felt like a funeral. I had to die to the idea that Kimberly would ever be the mom I'd hoped she would be to me.

I did wonder if all the problems I had with Kimberly would follow me into other relationships. I'd addressed my codependency, but now I had to see if I could escape it. I could move countries, but if my problems followed me, that would mean I was still the problem.

When we moved from Minnesota to Ohio, we fit all our belongings from a three-thousand-square-foot house into a duplex tucked in between the downtown post office and other historic houses. I didn't anticipate how much I would enjoy sitting on my porch, watching as people strolled along. Observing without knowing the context about where anyone was going or what anyone was doing dazzled me. Cars drove by. People walked to work. Kids rode their bikes. Neighbors chatted through long goodbyes, all while the porch held me.

Because I'd spent most of my life basing my decisions on what others deemed most accepted or admirable, I'd once thought we should live in the country on a farm. As

I understood it, the most Christian womanly choice was to homestead where my children could frolic and farm. So I'd considered the duplex a layover until that dream came to pass. But the porch would not let me go. It hugged me, giving me permission to be still while everything else buzzed and moved by. During this time, I discovered that I loved telling my children to "love their neighbors" while actually having neighbors to love. My son made a best friend next door. Jacob and I became judges at our neighbor's annual chili cook-off. Our family became so close with the tenants who lived in the other half of our duplex that we even celebrated Thanksgiving together. After about a year of getting to know our tenant and asking her to come to church with us, she came. On the same day, she dedicated her life to Jesus, received a Bible, and got Bibles for her daughters—the first Bibles they had ever owned. She's been coming to our church ever since. Watching her in the joy of her salvation helped me regain the joy of my own salvation. Being tucked in the heart of town replenished my depleted heart.

The community environment was a greenhouse for growth. Smothered in unconditional love, I could discover what God wanted from me rather than what others wanted and expected. Up until this point, my life had been a series of reactions. When we are codependent, we live by reacting to what we believe others want from us. I had made choices that I thought would make people love me, but moving away helped me learn how to make decisions for myself in a way that served God.

It is nearly impossible to heal in the environment where we are being or have been hurt.

I've heard that moving does not solve one's problems, but it solved many of ours.

To be honest, I wish we had done it sooner. I imagine things might not have gotten as bad as they did—but for so long, I interpreted leaving as the opposite of loving. I now understand that leaving felt like abandonment because so many people left me in my childhood. But sometimes leaving *is* a loving act, because it is nearly impossible to heal in the environment where we are being or have been hurt.

When Jacob and I became foster parents, one of my hopes was to be the kind of adult I needed when I was a kid. Being that person for the kids in my care is truly a gift to me, and I think the sentiment "Be who you needed" is generally a good one. However, amid our fostering experiences, and as I have healed, I have realized that sometimes this sentiment is not always for the best.

This sentiment can make loving and serving others about our own experiences rather than someone else's individual experience. If we focus primarily on our own childhood stories, we may become who *we* needed but not who the other person needs. I have learned through a lot of heartbreak that the people we serve are not pawns or pathways toward "healing our inner child." Can I be honest and say I don't even believe in healing my inner child? At least, I can't go back and reparent myself. I can and should reflect, process, and grieve what has happened to me, but imagining myself sitting there with little girl Tori and trying to parent her—giving myself what I need—has not helped me. However, accepting God as my Father, the one who is reparenting me in my adulthood, has been immensely healing.

What I've experienced and observed is that when we focus too much on what we needed when we were kids, we don't realize that we (and those around us) might need something different here and now. We might miss how God is working in our lives and giving us what we need today. Indeed, he is doing a new thing. We are different people than we were as kids, so we will need different things. Instead, we should ask: "What do I need for today?" This question can apply to ourselves *and* the people around us.

With that being said, if there's someone in your life who tears you down so much that it prevents you from bearing the cross you've been called to bear—marriage, parenthood, your vocation, or anything else—you can leave. Not because it does not serve you, but because it does not serve God.

Romans 16:17 says, "I urge you, brothers and sisters, to watch out for those who cause divisions and put obstacles in your way that are contrary to the teaching you have learned. Keep away from them." This scripture shows us that we have permission to set boundaries as followers of Jesus. We are allowed to step away from those who cause division, especially when that division prevents us from doing what God has called us to. Leaving in this capacity doesn't make us unloving or unkind. It is necessary. It makes us wise. And even though it is so hard, it can also be so healing.

LIKE JESUS, YOU CAN WALK AWAY

Jesus himself created boundaries many times. Jesus walked away for his own rest and away from people who betrayed him.[2] The lesson we can learn from this is that we do not have to feel guilty when we walk away. Actually, sometimes following in the footsteps of Jesus means walking away from others or letting them walk away from us.

After Jesus made others uncomfortable by preaching about eating his flesh and drinking his blood, he lost a lot of enthusiastic followers.[3] Instead of chasing them down and begging them not to misunderstand him, or doing what was necessary to make them come back, Jesus turned to the Twelve and essentially said, "So, what about you?"[4] With this question Jesus never appeared desperate, manipulative, or controlling. He never coerced his disciples to stay. He simply inquired with confidence.

Jesus valued his relationships. He loved people well. Loving was his entire purpose, but his love for others never compromised his identity. He never strayed left or right from who God called him to be and what God called him to do for the sake of others. He fulfilled his ultimate call, sacrificing his life on the cross for us *as a result of* being betrayed and hurt. Despite the rejection he received, he was who God called him to be and walked in accordance with God's will—which in turn made him the ultimate example of love.

In Scripture Judas was known for turning against Jesus and planting a kiss on him in the garden of Gethsemane. With that kiss he identified Jesus to the Jewish authorities who were looking to kill him—setting into motion Jesus' arrest, his trial, his death by crucifixion, and eventually his resurrection. The Christian faith was founded upon this series of events, which culminated in the resurrection and demonstrated the power of Christ to save humanity.

Despite knowing that Judas was going to betray him, Jesus washed Judas's feet and included him in the Last Supper, feeding him alongside the other disciples. Despite the ways Judas would break Jesus' heart, Jesus loved and cared for him. However, Jesus did not try to convince Judas not to leave or betray him because, ultimately, Jesus knew that the way Judas would hurt him would lead to the fulfillment of his purpose. Jesus did not love simply to be loved in return, but to point people toward his heavenly Father. Jesus was not willing to sacrifice the call God had on his life for the approval of man, and we shouldn't either.

God has called us to love—not for our glory but for his. Sometimes what we perceive as love is not love at all if it hinders us from doing what God has called us to. Your call to love others may require you to love even though you have been betrayed by those closest to you. Your call to love others may require you to leave. It may require you to wash the feet of those who have hurt you. Then it may require you to let them walk away so you can walk into exactly what God has called you to.

As unhealed, codependent people, we will do anything to grow or maintain a relationship. We attempt to rectify our broken childhoods and unhealthy histories by seeking new relationships that reflect the past relationships that hurt us most. We do not leave, and we do everything possible to please people so they will not walk away from us. But by doing that, we can so easily leave God. Jesus, however, was never willing to walk away from God. He was never outside of God's will and never far from him.

Some people would rather lose us than be honest about what they've done to us, and if that is the case, we can learn to let them go. We cannot rectify toxic relationships with our abusers by entering new toxic relationships. Attempting to make abusive people love us will inevitably result in failure. The only relationship that can and will heal us is an intimate relationship with God.

Judas's relationship with Jesus was special, but Jesus knew it would be detrimental to compel Judas to accept him, stay with him, and choose him. Instead, Jesus was sold out and dependent on the word of his Father. That's who he chased after.

We do not need to chase those who are not chasing us. Perhaps it's time to stop running, take a breather, and look around. Who did we lose along the way while we were busy pursuing those who never even gave us the first glance?

GOD STAYS

After I moved back to my hometown, I went to Tonya's house nearly every night. Whenever I went to her house, I felt like my body and mind could rest. I talked with her for hours, and sometimes we sat in silence. It had been months since I'd spent time with her like that. Then, before I'd walk out the front door, I'd sometimes look at her and say, "You have to be so sick of me." A normal person would agree, but Tonya would giggle, gently hug me, and whisper, "Never." For a while I thought she was just saying that because she didn't want to make me feel bad. But if a week passed and I didn't come over, she'd say, "Man, I missed you," or "I've been wondering where you've been and when you'd come back."

God welcomes each of us in the same way. He can listen to us talk endlessly. He can sit with us quietly. Then, when we become honest with him, we think he must really know us—which means he must really be tired of us too. Yet he isn't. He is still delighted to be with us.

After so many times of experiencing our God's delight in us, we become convinced that maybe, just maybe, we are beloved ourselves. We become more of a delight because we so easily become what we are perceived to be.

These days I don't go to Tonya's as much as I used to, even though we only live half a mile away from each other. But I'm very thankful for that season when she let me show up so often. Our time together healed me. And after that year, I felt like much of my anger shattered and my capacity to love—especially for mothers—grew. My perspective began to shift, and my compassion and understanding for even Kimberly began to expand. My heart was softened by Tonya's soft landing.

A piece of me needed a mom to be with me and love me so I could be a better mom to my kids. That year, because I chose to leave the place where I was stuck, I showed up and let myself be loved. As I opened myself up to loving others again, I healed.

I now know the fear of leaving people was a part of my codependency and my deeper fear of abandonment. Staying put worked very well for me, until it did not.

The people-pleasing child in each of us got us this far, so truly we don't need to shame ourselves for these patterns of behavior. Actually we should applaud and honor that little person for the survival mechanisms they developed. Then we can acknowledge the patterns that can be changed for the better.

At the end of the day, we will not face other people in heaven. We will be locking eyes with Christ, and we will want to say with certainty, "I did what God wanted me to do, not what people wanted me to do. I did what was pleasing to my Father—the one who never left me." We cannot be everything to everyone, because then we could not be all God called us to be. Galatians 1:10 says, "Am I now trying to win the approval of human beings, or of God? Or am I trying to please people? If I were still trying to please people, I would not be a servant of Christ." Sometimes the best way to find who and how God wants us to love is to leave. I don't want to waste my life chasing people who wouldn't take two steps toward me. I want to spend this life chasing God.

LIE 13

YOU'RE NOT READY YET

WHEN I WAS THIRTEEN, I LIVED IN A GROUP HOME WITH nine other young women who had experienced immense trauma. One girl named Libby lived in the bedroom across from me. Her hair went one way and then the other, just like her eyes. At night when we were supposed to be in bed, she would escape her room and set off the alarms. Libby would then come to our closed doors, lie on the ground, and speak to us through the crack between the floor and our door, trying to convince us to come out and wreak havoc with her. We were instructed not to talk to her when she had one of these episodes, but whenever she came to my door, I couldn't help myself. I'd grab my Bible and read her some verses that I found encouraging.

I was not a professing or practicing Christian at this point, but like I did when I was in juvie, I read my Bible when I had nothing else to do in the group home.

I went to church because I thought I could earn my way out of the group home by going. If I went to church, I thought, God would see it as "enough" to grant me a family. Though I did not understand the true meaning of church or what it meant to love Christ, I invited the other girls in the group home to come to church along with me. The staff often said they'd never had a group of girls going to church as consistently as ours did.

When a girl started to throw a tantrum, which happened daily, I would whisper, "Slow to anger." It did not work every time, but many times I could calm the girls down quicker with these words than the staff could. I say this not to boast, but because when I look back, I see something in myself that believed I had authority to teach the Word and encourage people with it. I imagine that was God, who I believe was always within me, stirring my heart, pursuing me, and showing me what I would someday do.

Now I get to mentor and mother young women who have lived lives like mine and the other young women in that group home. I teach Scripture and encourage people with the Bible, sometimes in small groups and sometimes through books and sometimes from stages. When I look back at how this happened, I see God moving at many points in my life despite the fact that I was young and untrained. My intention was not vocational ministry as much as it was to tell people what God had done in my life.

At the age of seventeen I was given my first speaking engagement. When I was eighteen I began helping with Bible studies at my college. When I was twenty I did a ministry internship at my church. By twenty-one I was in an outreach ministry working for a nonprofit. By the time I was twenty-two, I was writing and speaking full-time in ministry. I had been saved for not even a year when I entered ministry, and many people have told me since then that I "started young."

I received much encouragement from empathic listeners and heard many testimonies from people who were encouraged amid their own hardships whenever I shared my story—but I also heard a competing narrative that said I wasn't ready for ministry. I heard I just needed more time to "get there." Wanting to know exactly how I could grow, I asked a naysayer for guidance. And he said, "I just know from my experience in ministry that these things are supposed to happen in a certain order. It takes time."

However, when Paul was called by God, he admitted that he did not consult anyone or take much time off. Instead, Paul very quickly set off to do what God had called him to do. In Galatians 1:15–16, Paul stated, "When God, who set me apart from my mother's womb and called me by his grace, was pleased to reveal his Son in me so that I might preach him among the Gentiles, my immediate response was not to consult any human being." Paul didn't need the permission of anyone but God. Likewise, you do not need permission from anyone except God to fulfill the purpose he has set you apart for.

After Paul set off without consulting anyone about what he felt his mission was, he went from city to city to city. Finally he testified about what God did through his work when he said, "They praised God because of me."[1]

When people say we aren't ready, what they don't see is how God can fill in the gaps. My experience—stepping into ministry, being in the church, being surrounded by other ministers, and sharing my testimony—brought me closer to God. My character was more refined because of the environment I was in than it would have been had I waited.

USE YOUR GIFTS

Our greatest mission is the Great Commission, which can be carried out from a cash register, the floor of a restaurant, an office desk, a stage, or anywhere else. But because part of my mission was on a stage, I felt insecure to claim it. I thought it would look prideful if I did. I thought, *What makes me think I deserve any platform, let alone a stage?*

I expressed concern to a wise mentor of mine, and she directed me toward Romans 12, which says:

> For by the grace given to me I say to everyone among you not to think of himself more highly than he ought to think, but to think with sober judgment, each according to the measure of faith that God has assigned. For as in one body we have many members, and the members do not all have the same function, so we, though many, are one body in Christ, and individually members one of another. Having gifts that differ

according to the grace given to us, let us use them: if proph-
ecy, in proportion to our faith; if service, in our serving; the
one who teaches, in his teaching; the one who exhorts, in his
exhortation; the one who contributes, in generosity; the one
who leads, with zeal; the one who does acts of mercy, with
cheerfulness.[2]

Then my mentor said, "It only becomes prideful when you
forget your gift is a gift." Furthermore, this scripture reminds
us that not one gift is considered greater than the other. The
world might admire teaching and speaking more than unseen
service, but God sees them as the same—so when others make
too much of our gifts in a way that makes us feel unworthy
of them, we can remember that God sees only our faith and
works through our willing hearts.

Now, this pattern of thinking did not instantly go away
for me. At times I still struggled to embrace the gifts God had
given me, and one of my other mentors, Danielle, addressed
me about it. When I shared my hesitations and doubts with
her, she said, "Humility is simply agreeing with who God says
you are." Or, to revisit what Paul wrote in Romans 12:3: "I say
to everyone among you not to think of himself more highly
than he ought to think, but to think with sober judgment"
(ESV). Humility is not making ourselves less or more of who
God has called us to be. Humility is showing up as God calls
us to.

Then I attended a conference where speakers shared their
life stories and what they'd learned from them. Over and over,

I heard testimonies and stories that pricked my heart. Each story helped me see a piece of myself I had yet to understand.

In the middle of one talk, I felt overwhelmed and decided I needed a break. I felt a heavy weight on my soul. I walked to the restroom, stood in front of the mirror, and when I looked at myself, tears started to roll down my face. I didn't hear the audible voice of God, but I felt something in my gut. It said, *If you don't share your testimony, you are wasting what God has done. Everyone has a story worth telling.* Now, I'm not sure God's glory and power and goodness could even be wasted. I don't think we have the power to do such a thing, but I do think we can cover up our own light. And I do believe that God does a marvelous job of meeting us where we are and communicating in words and ways we understand. And with those words, in that restroom, I understood what I needed to do next. My testimony of what God had done in my life was a light within me, and I needed to stop covering it up out of fear of what others would think.

In 2 Corinthians Paul addressed this very topic to those who were posing as apostles. Paul was speaking about himself when he wrote, "I consider myself in no way inferior to those 'super-apostles.' Even if I am untrained in public speaking, I am certainly not untrained in knowledge."[3] Paul addressed the naysayers, acknowledging that he may not have had all the talents they expected him to—but he had what mattered. Other people might not have considered Paul to be qualified or ready, but Paul did not let that stop him. And we shouldn't let it stop us either.

Those naysayers' voices could have crushed me. I could have doubted what I heard, but I remembered that when people measure you by where you came from and not by your identity as a new creation in Christ, their measurement is inaccurate. Only God can determine our readiness. God does not measure our character by human standards. God sees differently than man. When we come into a relationship with God, we become his sons and daughters, which means we inherit his gifts. On Christmas morning, we don't open a great gift and put it back under the tree. We fiddle with it and learn how to use it better. We use the gifts we are given, and we can do the same with the gifts God has given us.

GO AND TELL

Nearly four years after I shared my testimony for the first time, I received a message on Instagram that said, "We heard your story at your church, and that night we took the step to get involved in foster care, and today we are adopting a sibling group because of it." I was seventeen when I shared my testimony for the first time, and according to some, I was not "ready." I was not "mature enough." And I definitely wasn't "healed enough." But the testimony wasn't about me being enough. The work we do isn't about how mature, healed, and great we are. It's not about us being ready, equipped, or prepared. Rather, when we put our stories and our willing hearts to use for God, it becomes about how enough *he* is. It is about how great he is. And God prepares the people we serve to receive.

Very well. I may not have been "ready," but God's people were. To say I was not ready, then, is to say those kids shouldn't have been adopted at that time. To say I was not healed enough to do what God had called me to do is to say a family shouldn't have stepped in to serve orphans when they did. Stepping into our callings compels others to step into theirs. That doesn't guarantee we are doing it perfectly, but what a joy to serve the Lord while a little wobbly rather than not at all.

Though I surely was not healed before telling my story publicly, sharing my story healed me. Statistics say many of my peers, those who have grown up similarly to me, are using drugs, alcohol, and other harmful means to heal and numb the pain.[4] So I want to kindly caution leaders who see someone like me and think, *They're not ready to tell their story*: Do not label them as such. Even though I was young, sharing my story was an alternative to other means of coping—and God used my storytelling to help me heal.

I would argue that sharing my story was one of the most unexpected and underrated steps I took toward my healing. When people ask about my healing journey they expect me to talk about therapy, community, relationships, and other modalities, but telling my story has been a critical part of my journey. This is because studies show that when we tell our stories to empathetic listeners, our brain chemistry changes the way we view ourselves and each other.[5] When heard with compassion, we can go from seeing ourselves with shame to seeing ourselves as understood, strong, capable, and loved. Soon we even begin to take pride in our stories.

As I share my story from the stage, I am often speaking to hundreds and sometimes thousands of compassionate listeners at a time. God has used this process and these many empathetic listeners to heal my brain, body, and broken heart.

As Revelation 12:11 says, "They triumphed over him by the blood of the Lamb and by the word of their testimony." We overcome through sharing the testimony of what God has done in our lives.

Storytelling helps us process what has happened to us, in the same way one would speak with a counselor or friend. When we revisit the past through storytelling, it is nearly impossible not to see how God was there in the midst of our struggles. When we tell our stories, our eyes are opened to God's faithfulness and closeness along the journey. And when we share our testimonies, people respond with their own testimonies. Every time I share, I witness the worst parts of my story being made good. For years I've gotten to hear how my story has helped someone else. When we go and tell, others go and tell, which makes others go and tell. Storytelling breeds storytelling. Vulnerability breeds vulnerability. Stepping into our callings encourages others to be brave, despite their not-enoughness, and step into what they've been called to do.

> When we go and tell, others go and tell, which makes others go and tell.

Healing begins and continues in our lives because of the stories we tell and the stories we hear.

In Scripture Jesus tells people to go and share, to tell what he has done in their lives. And it is no coincidence that this modern modality called *therapy*, which our generation finds so healing, involves telling our stories.

Jesus believed stories were important too.

Mark 5 tells the story of a demon-possessed man living in a cave where the dead were buried. Though the man could not be restrained, Jesus healed the man—and once he was healed he went from demon-possessed to "perfectly sane." The bewildered bystanders who had seen this maddened man wreaking havoc were shocked by the miracle of Jesus. The witnesses did not walk but *ran* to the nearby towns and the surrounding area, spreading the news and telling the story of Jesus' miracle.

Jesus then went to leave, and as he was getting into his boat, the man Jesus had healed begged to go with Jesus. The man wanted to walk, learn, and live beside Jesus too. And Jesus, having one will with God, doing all things on earth for the glory of his heavenly Father, responded to the man and said, "No, go home to your family, and tell them everything the Lord has done for you and how merciful he has been." Instead of inviting this man along, Jesus encouraged the man to go and share his testimony.

The following verse says, "So the man started off to visit the Ten Towns of that region and began to proclaim the great things Jesus had done for him; and everyone was amazed at what he told them."[6]

What is so incredible about this story is that even though plenty of other people had witnessed this miracle and told the story, and though even more people would likely continue to tell the story, Jesus told the man he healed to share his own story to his community and family. Rather than asking the man to come along so he might become "ready" or "more healed" or "more equipped," Jesus found it most valuable for the man to go and tell his story right then and there.

The man was healed, and his witness was a testament of what Jesus had done. He did not have to muster his own human greatness to do the work of God, because Jesus had already told him what to do. Jesus did not tell the man that he needed to do x, y, and z to get ready to do the work of God. He simply needed to go and tell because his witness was enough. His story would give others hope that they, their family members, and their friends could heal too. Ultimately, his miraculous story would bring people to the healing power of Jesus. Then the formerly demon-possessed man, now a saint, would discover even greater healing and hope as he watched his words heal and bring hope to others. He would walk with Jesus in his heart, even though he did not walk with Jesus on foot. This man is an example to each of us to go and tell of what God has done in our lives, even if we don't feel quite ready.

If God opens the door, be brave enough to walk through it. Rest assured that the learning experience to come will make you more like Christ than you would have become had you shut the door and waited to be ready. First Timothy 4:12 says, "Do not let anyone treat you as if you are unimportant because you are young. Instead, be an example to the believers with your words, your actions, your love, your faith, and your pure life" (NCV). So I urge you, do not listen to the naysayers who use your age or experience to discourage you from starting.

If you are a parent, you know it is normal to mature and grow as we raise our children. I become a better parent because I continually parent. I do not become more Christlike in my motherhood by shutting down or waiting until I am "ready" to be a better mom. It's the same with any vocation. Of course we aim for a general level of maturity, but our vocations and God-given purposes refine us as we continue to engage in them.

You've probably heard plenty of people sharing their stories from the other side, when it looks like they have it all together. But whenever I share my story while I'm still hurting—while I'm in the midst of my unreadiness and healing—it shows others they are not alone. When the story isn't about how great we are, we all feel more human, and then we can point people to God. To love is to tell the story when we aren't "ready" or healed, so those around us have others to heal alongside—not just people pointing fingers and telling them how.

When we tell the story of Jesus, we realize we are not just battered, depressed, and broken people. We are chosen witnesses of God's love. We have seen, tasted, and heard that God does a good job writing stories, and if he did a good job writing *that* story, he will do a good job writing the one we're in.

You might never speak from stages or write books. Not all of us are called to be storytellers vocationally, but all of us have stories worth telling. In our communities, across our tables, in our dining rooms, and in our small groups—let's tell stories for the sake of everyone's healing. It would be a waste of time to wait until we feel ready.

The one who believes we have to prepare to speak of God's goodness writes these words off as heresy, but the one who has witnessed God showing up in weakness and brokenness smiles. That person knows human readiness is not the mark.

Now hear me. I do want to add a caveat. Impulsivity is a trauma response, and at certain times, Jesus urged the ones he had healed and the crowds who saw it not to tell anyone. For example, in Mark 1: "Jesus sternly charged him and sent him away at once, and said to him, 'See that you say nothing to anyone, but go, show yourself to the priest and offer for your cleansing what Moses commanded, for a proof to them.'"[7] People talking about Jesus' miracles drew crowds, and sometimes it made it hard for Jesus to go to his next destination. Every time we go on mission or go and tell, we should prayerfully discern if that is what God wants us to do—but we do not need man's validation when we have God's approval.

> We do not need man's validation when we have God's approval.

Before stepping into ministry or any purposeful work, we should aim to look like Christ in character. When we proclaim Jesus' name but look like the opposite, we do damage to our witness. But we do not have to be ready by the world's standards to accept what God has called us to. We do not have to be perfect and poised to step into our purpose.

YOU ARE READY

I would never say or believe that God placed me in ministry because I am particularly gifted. I believe this mission and purpose is a gift God has given me to keep me tethered to him, and because my story has helped me care for the people Jesus cares for.

I have talked about much of the work I get to do as vocational or public ministry, but I also believe ministry can be the ordinary, everyday acts of loving our neighbor, serving the poor, and caring for the orphan and the widow.[8] As Christians, we are invited to live our entire lives as if we are on mission to glorify God and guide people toward his love. We can invite people into our homes, make conversation with the person checking us out at the grocery store, seek and advocate for justice for the oppressed, and demonstrate Jesus through almost any of our regular actions.

Recently, I have been trying to help a human trafficking survivor escape from her trafficker. We connected after she was given resources by an organization that my husband and I volunteer for, but our bond formed so seamlessly because she, too, is a former foster youth.

Though we have similar backgrounds, communication

has not always been easy between us. I can't always respond as quickly as she would like me to, and I don't always say what she wants to hear. Then she berates me, calling me names and accusing me of not caring about her.

Do you remember earlier in the book when I told you I sent verbally abusive text messages to Kimberly? Well, it wasn't until I met this human trafficking survivor that I realized how those words actually made someone feel. I realized that I had done something very similar to others—not just hoping they would help me but expecting them to be the ones to heal me.

When we were first foster parents, a young man left our home, screaming that we were kicking him out though we never had. That, too, made me realize I'd done the same thing to my dad when I was in college. Only when I became a mom did I begin to have more compassion for my mom and other mother figures who I once felt had failed me. Since serving others who have grown up like me and stepping into different roles, I have gained more knowledge and perspective. And I wouldn't have gained that knowledge had I waited to serve. I think the experience to show up in places we once needed to be served in is usually a greater gift to us than it is to those we are serving because of the knowledge we gain.

Those of us who choose to serve others with similar backgrounds and similar pain, who have been through the fire and walk out of the flames carrying buckets of water for those still consumed, haven't waited until we are ready by the world's standards. We see the fire and can't watch our neighbors burning. That doesn't mean our aim is always perfect when we throw the water or that our buckets are always full, but we should be proud of ourselves nonetheless. We are not willing to watch God's children suffer. Through the fire and through the fight, we may get burned—but we will definitely gain strength, endurance, and knowledge as we help others.

We can't let others kill the purpose God has for us. Pursuing a purpose in Christ and being on mission for God in all things will purify and make you ready, because we learn and become more experienced and knowledgeable by doing. You are as ready as you'll ever be right here and right now.

LIE 14

YOU NEED CLOSURE
TO HEAL

AT THE AGE OF SIXTEEN I WAS IN MY ELEVENTH FOS-
ter home, living with a younger married couple. To the people
in town, they appeared perfect and were even admired. But
behind closed doors they brutally abused one of their adopted
sons. Eventually, I reported my foster mom for pouring feces
on the boy's head and making their rottweiler attack him. Very
sadly, but not to my surprise at all, the report was deemed false
and I was labeled a liar.

Ever since then, I have hoped for some form of justice for
that boy. He remained in the home and continued to experience years of abuse and neglect, which were swept under the
rug by caseworkers, neighbors, and family members. On top
of that, he was blamed for the dysfunction in the home.

Though I wanted a rescue mission for this boy, as a

teenager in foster care I had no power to make a difference in the system or in his life. And because I was so powerless, I decided the only means I had to obtain any power of my own was to forgive the perpetrators. If I forgave them, they had no control over my emotions. When I saw them in public, I could maintain my peace. When I heard their names, I could not speak ill about them. I had peace as long as it was up to me.

Eventually I moved away, so I didn't see or think of them too often. But about ten years after I had moved from that home, the foster father requested to connect with me on social media. I was instantly taken aback when I saw his face pop up on my screen. My knee-jerk reaction was to not allow him into my life, in even the smallest way online.

But during this time, I happened to be studying the book of Romans, and this passage came to mind:

> Repay no one evil for evil, but give thought to do what is honorable in the sight of all. If possible, so far as it depends on you, live peaceably with all. Beloved, never avenge yourselves, but leave it to the wrath of God, for it is written, "Vengeance is mine, I will repay, says the Lord." To the contrary, "if your enemy is hungry, feed him; if he is thirsty, give him something to drink; for by doing so you will heap burning coals on his head." Do not be overcome by evil, but overcome evil with good.[1]

If you are like me, after someone has done something so unjust and hurtful, the idea of heaping burning coals on their head sounds about right. So after some thought, I accepted his friend request for the opportunity to overcome evil with good and for the opportunity to be so kind that he felt burning coals.

I also accepted his request because I was in a healthy enough space at this point and expected nothing from him. I knew what God said about me: I was loved, and their rejection was my protection. And I knew what God said about the situation: He loved his children, and they were not to be treated with abuse, but with protection. I never needed closure or reassurance from that foster father or mother, but I had a feeling that this request was the closure *he* needed to resolve the trauma and emotional damage.

Within minutes, a message from him appeared in my inbox. I took a deep breath before opening the casual greeting he sent.

Then, after just a few back-and-forth messages, he apologized for what happened in the home. Though he was never physically abusive, he was a passive endorser. He had more power than the rest of us kids and never put a stop to the abuse. Nonetheless, I told him I forgave him, but that I'd written a book in which he wasn't portrayed as a good character. He responded by saying, "That's okay. I deserve that."

A few days later, I briefly met him in person to give him a copy of *Fostered*, my memoir about my first twenty-four years, which included the story of living in his home. I didn't expect a response from him. More so, I expected him to be upset at what I had written, go silent, and return to avoiding the truth.

But he messaged me just one day later and said he'd read my entire memoir in a day. Then he confirmed that he remembered much of what I wrote about. He proceeded to apologize again.

Closure is defined by a feeling that an emotional or traumatic experience has been resolved, and many of us yearn for it after we have been hurt. At an earlier moment, while I was in college, I thought it would be a good idea to have dinner with an ex-boyfriend so we could find some closure—but if I'm honest with myself, that wasn't what I was looking for. I was looking for validation and even the possibility to rekindle the relationship. See, "seeking closure" can be dangerous because it can lead us right back to the places where we were dysfunctional and unhealthy.

I understand why closure can help us feel better about a hard situation, but I also want you to understand that when we determine that peace is up to us, we can bring closure to the situation without the risk of falling back into old patterns. When I decided to forgive my abusive foster parents, I became free. I could have spent years hoping my foster dad would bring closure in the form of a confession and an apology. But I didn't need the apology or a conversation labeled "closure," because I knew God saw what happened. And I knew what God had spoken over my identity.

This doesn't mean we should not lean into difficult conversations that could lead to resolution, but I caution against seeking closure in heavily dysfunctional relationships with a history of damaging patterns. Remember: How people act and what people do reveals more about their character than what they say. Even though we may long for an apology or a confession from certain people, such conversations can also lead us back to dysfunctional people and dysfunctional relationships. And sometimes, like in my situation, these conversations aren't even available to us; some people will never be willing to confess and apologize. In this case, we can let people's patterns speak for themselves. After all, patterns speak louder than words.

If we think we can't experience healing without closure, that means we are letting other people's actions determine the posture of our hearts. But when we rest in knowing that God alone knows the truth of people's actions, we can truly be set free. While my foster father's confession and apology brought me more peace, I did not need his apology to move on and experience healing. My healing has come from seeing one's actions for what they are, knowing that God knows all, and knowing God.

I used to long for closure, but when this was not available to me, I began to see the value in the old saying "Actions speak louder than words." Now I see people's actions as a form of closure as well. Someone lying to cover up abuse can give us the closure we desire. Abusers blaming victims is a form of closure. Silence and nonresponses are forms of closure. A person refusing to confess and take responsibility for their corrupt and unjust actions is a form of closure. Patterns speak louder than promises, and a person continually acting in a harmful way points us to the truth of their character. We don't have to keep searching for more resolution. We don't need conversations about a relationship wherein consistent abusive and destructive patterns continue. Let people's actions close the door, and let God's protection seal the lock. He knows the truth, and his knowing is closure enough.

GOD'S PROMISES ARE WAITING FOR YOU

The experience with my foster father caused me to stop seeking closure from others, because closure from God is far greater. His apologies and confessions reminded me, and continually remind me, of God's promises: He sees it all, and he will prepare a table before you in the presence of your enemies. Then he will anoint your head with oil while your cup overflows.[2]

At one point I would have guessed the table was a fancy place to show my foster father how far I'd come without him. I thought the overflow would be my successes and accolades, but now I know the overflow I was able to offer my foster father was a kindness and forgiveness I couldn't have given on my own. It was there for him before he ever apologized, and it would have been there if he never did, all because of God's kindness and forgiveness toward me. The table set for me was one where he could see I sat with God—a God who would invite him and set his table too.

LET'S BE PEOPLE WHO APOLOGIZE

This is not to say apologies aren't valuable and healing. About a year ago I spoke at a group home I used to live in. When

I lived there as a young person, part of the "programming" involved a point system. If we did something "good," we would be rewarded with a thousand positive points to write down and record on a piece of paper. But if we did something bad, the consequence was losing three thousand or more points.

When other girls lost points, they often did not care. Some would even continue the behavior to antagonize the staff for laughs. But when I lost points, I heard my mom's voice. I'd go upstairs in my room, shut the door, and cry. I'd write in my journal over and over, "I will be better. I will do better." By myself, I would then rehearse how to react to the situation the way they wanted me to so I wouldn't lose points again. Most of the girls I lived with received multiple negative consequences a day. On a bad week for me, I maybe received one penalty. Because criticism crushed me, I tried to avoid it at all costs.

From a trauma-informed perspective, I have come to disagree with that kind of programming. Though I appreciate this home for being one of the safest places I ever lived, their programming did not work for me. If anything, it heaped trauma on top of my trauma. However, I was never abused, nor did I ever witness abuse by any of the staff. I received much-needed counseling services and was offered many opportunities through sports, extracurricular activities, and education, which I was not offered in some foster homes. I could see that much of what they had done was good, so it was relatively easy to forgive them. I genuinely believe that when it came to the poor programming, they simply did not understand what they were doing.

Before the speaking engagement for them, I went to lunch with the staff. Many of those I ate with were once my caregivers and overseers while I lived there. It was clear they saw me with great love and respect. They continually told me they were proud of me. Though I never brought it up, they broached the subject of the point system, and tears began to well in their eyes. One of the staff members started off the lunch by admitting that she recognized the programming was harmful to me, and she apologized individually and on behalf of the organization.

While I had already forgiven them, their apology made me trust them all the more. It has made my love for each person there grow, and most importantly, it made my heart rest assured that my guess was correct: They simply did not have the resources and knowledge we have today, but they are still learning and aspiring to care for kids.

These days, our family goes to the organization regularly to spend time with the young men living there. (They transitioned to an all-boys campus.) We eat dinner together, play games with them, and bring them ice cream. The leadership of the organization offered our family the opportunity to learn to ride horses at their facility after we finish hanging out with the young men on our visits. My kids have loved it, and every time we go, I can't help but become overwhelmed with emotion and gratitude. This home was one of the safest places I lived as a kid, and it's one of our family's safest places now.

We can experience this kind of healing and redemption through forgiveness long before an apology occurs. Then, when an apology *is* made, the act deepens our trust for that person. It would have been easy to harden my heart against the home, say no to the speaking engagement, and miss the redemption.

Our family, the boys who live in the home, the staff, and I could have missed all of this, but we made a choice to say yes to humility. Yes to togetherness. Yes to reopened doors. Yes to an apology. Yes to forgiveness.

The best form of closure we have to offer comes in the form of forgiveness. And the best part is, forgiveness is a step we can take even when our hearts are hurting. Forgiveness relieves the pain, bitterness, and anger that can so easily resurface. To this day, I've never received an apology in which true responsibility was taken by those who have hurt me the most. Still, I forgive them. But because I know the hurt of not being apologized to, and because a huge part of me continues to hope for their repentance, I choose to apologize to others often.

> God's heart skips a beat when we choose to apologize.

Let's be people who humbly apologize when we are in the wrong. Apologies are a real depiction of God being made strong in our own weakness. I believe that God's heart skips a beat when we choose to apologize.

When we are aware of how we have been hurt, we don't wish to hurt others; but when we fall short and do hurt others, it is important to muster the humility to apologize. In our home, my husband and I apologize to each other and our kids often. Apologies make us face our shortcomings. Then, when others have shortcomings, they are easier to forgive because we remember our own. Can I invite you to consider who you may need to apologize to? Might you consider who you can forgive to bring yourself the closure and healing you have been yearning for?

TRUTH

You Are a Pattern Breaker

I HAVE SEEN PEOPLE STEP AWAY FROM RELATIONSHIPS to heal. For them, it's what they need to begin to change the unhealthy patterns they acquired in the relationship or while growing up. Sometimes parents or other family members will blame the person stepping away for the issues in the family, naming them "the problem." Some families will even refer to that person as a "prodigal child."

But there comes a time when you have done everything you can to heal and mend the relationship—at which point, you have permission to stop taking full responsibility for the problem.

Plus, an adult who has set boundaries with those who have proved themselves toxic is *not* a prodigal. A prodigal is not even an adult who steps away from authority figures or family in order to avoid dysfunction. This reference originates from one of Jesus' parables in Scripture—the story about a son who takes his father's inheritance and spends it on wild living. So, actually, *prodigal* is defined as someone who spends money or resources recklessly and wastefully. But someone who steps away to change the course of their unhealthy patterns? That is a cycle breaker. Many of us who are called "prodigals" really aren't. We are breaking generational patterns others have yet to acknowledge.

Often, people will react negatively to our change because they have benefited from our patterns staying the same. Some people will be upset about your healing process because you were easier to control when you *weren't* healing.

On top of this, in an unhealthy relationship dynamic, the healthiest person (the pattern breaker) can appear to be the cause of the conflict. Whether they are choosing not to show up or they are pointing out the dysfunction or they are simply trying to disrupt "the way we have always done things," their actions are perceived as hostile. But that doesn't mean the cycle breaker isn't doing what is right. It's important to remember that change does not usually come without challenge and friction. Rest assured that you're not the problem as you break these patterns. You're not a prodigal. You're paving the way for generations to come.

WE CAN'T HEAL OURSELVES OUT OF BEING HUMAN

About two years had gone by since I'd seen Kimberly, but then our family was invited to an event her family would also be attending. While I wondered what our interaction might look like, for the first time in a year, I no longer cared to change myself in order to earn her approval. In the past, I would have tried to talk to her and present myself as if I had all the answers she wanted to hear. Then I'd wait for her praises and affirmation. But this time, I cared to be kind but not striving in her presence.

I read an article recently that stated, "Avoiding your triggers is not healing."[1] This is a faulty claim. You may have experienced healing while also remaining vulnerable to triggers. Many of our triggers are physiological, bodily eruptions that we cannot control. Our nervous systems are literally primed to react in ways that keep us safe, and those systems signal that we are in danger because of what we have experienced in the past. Therefore, staying away from our triggers can be part of breaking our patterns.

Think about it. We would not tell a recovering alcoholic to go to a bar. We would not tell a former drug addict to check out the local dispensary. We wouldn't take a friend with a gambling addiction to a casino. In relationships, the same can be true. If one has found themselves codependent, addicted to relationships the same way some are addicted to substances, might we suggest they keep their distance from those with whom they will make a trauma bond? Put simply, any and all addictions are idols we should be cautious of.

As we learn to navigate stress and fear in its various forms, and as we face those unavoidable triggers, we can commit to being kind to ourselves. Commit to forgiving yourself when you go into survival mode and react in ways you later regret. Rest assured, beloved, our trauma is not our identity no matter how we react. While my bodily eruptions have become less subtle for me, they still happen. I used to yell and cry when triggered, but on the day I had to face Kimberly, my body just shook. Having a reaction that is anything other than perfection does not mean your healing has taken millions of steps back. Nor does it mean you are some lost cause despite your efforts to heal. It simply means you're human.

I was cautious at the event as I felt my body shaking. At the beginning of the night, I pulled my husband into the bathroom, hugged him, and began to sob on his shoulder. As the tears fell, it felt like years' worth of pain falling away.

My husband gently asked, "Why are you feeling this?"

In between wails I cried, "I remember. I remember what she said about me, and all that she's done to me, and it just hurts." Jacob continued to hold me. Eventually my tears subsided, and I took a breath.

He continued to hold me, hold space for me, and stand quietly. I looked up at him, his hands around my waist, and smiled. "I'm okay. I think I just needed to cry it out." After I cried, I felt safer to approach the rest of the evening—almost like I just had to get it out. Researchers actually say that crying is like a release valve for our body. While crying can appear weak, crying is actually a way to combat repressive coping, which is the act of stuffing down all of our emotions and moving on. In other words, crying brings our bodies, brains, and hearts into equilibrium. Studies have shown that repressive coping can be linked to heart conditions, weaker immune systems, and several mental health conditions, including depression and anxiety. Crying, however, can signal real recovery.[2] Sometimes, to react is to heal.

We can't heal ourselves out of being human. We cannot transcend our humanity.

> We cannot transcend our humanity.

DANCE. RESTORATION IS COMING.

I believe it is no coincidence that what came as naturally to me as crying at the event was dancing. When the music came on, I couldn't help but dance. When we dance, that burst of happiness we feel is from the dopamine being released in our brains.[3] The amount of joy I had that night was unparalleled. I distinctly remember loving who I was created to be in front of people who seemed driven to mold me into something different. I was able to dance because old dreams of what life was supposed to look like had been released during my years of healing. My hands were open to reality, and in that reality, I felt a lightness I'd never experienced before. I knew myself. I knew God. I needed no one in that room to validate who I was.

We can move so much more freely when we know that nothing can separate us from God's loving-kindness. If you have not felt it or seen it, or if you've felt distant from it, return to his voice. Return to the truth. He builds us up. He restores us.

During my time of idolizing relationships and the voices of others, God's loving-kindness felt further away. When we depend upon others more than God, God's presence feels distant and we struggle to communicate with him. His voice is drowned out by the voices of others. Our sorrow and desperation for love continue to grow. We can't hear God like we once did.

But God chose us to be his children. We are not immune to suffering because of God, but his voice is the balm our wounds need to heal. His voice surely blesses us.

When David became king of Israel, one of the first things he did after defeating the Philistines was to place the ark of the covenant in his city. Because the ark functioned as a way for God to be present with the Israelites, David hoped having the ark nearby would bring blessings upon him. When the ark was returned, "David danced before the LORD with all his might, wearing a priestly garment."[4] Then all the people of Israel joined in shouting jubilantly and blowing horns. Having the ark allowed people to communicate with God and be in his presence once again—a gift that filled them with gratitude and joy.[5]

As you continue in your healing journey, there will be some days when you do not feel you can dance as freely as David. On other days, you will question the cycles you've broken. You will likely feel discouraged and bogged down on some days, but I invite you to come back here and remember the truths of what your Father says about you. Remember, too, that this healing journey is not linear or one-size-fits-all.

Healing is much more complex than any self-help or inspirational book can quite encompass. But on those days, I hope you remember to dance—and remember that no matter your tears or triggers or lingering reactions, God surely will continue to restore you.

Recently a woman who was about two decades older than me approached me at a speaking engagement and said, "I wish I was as healed as you are, but no matter what I do, I just can't heal." In the coming months or years, if you think the same about yourself, I want you to hear what I said to her. I said, "Do not look at someone else and gauge your healing by theirs. Rather, look behind you and compare your healing to who you were as a little child, a teenager, and a younger adult—the versions of you in all your past phases. Chances are, you've come a long way."

I used to think that if I had a bad reaction or if I was triggered, that meant I'd made no progress. But when I considered how I would have reacted a year prior or what my thought patterns would have been two years prior, I realized I *had* healed. From there, I threw away the idea that I need to have all the right reactions all the time. Instead, I found peace with how far I'd come, accepting that I would never be completely healed on this side of heaven. If real healing does happen, it will usually take time.

When Jacob and I restored our hundred-year-old duplex, the process was slow. And when we'd try to rush through a project, we usually had to go back and fix it again. Our healing journeys are the same. We can't hurry through them and expect the best results. But when we finished even the littlest project in that house, it was worth rejoicing over because we were one step closer to welcoming people into the safe home we'd envisioned.

Now, if I *had* to name a gauge of healing for us, I would say it's our ability to let people in, to hold them, and to be held. For me, healing has looked a lot like being hospitable and letting people be hospitable to me. It has looked like loving people into a safe house and being loved myself.

The first home that my husband and I restored is now a short-term rental that holds people when they travel through to visit family, enjoy a vacation, or attend funerals or events. My husband and I now live in a different, two-hundred-year-old home just down the street (we really love old homes), where we love to embrace our community and be embraced in return. And something I've noticed about the home we live in now is that it was restored and maintained really well. When we moved in, some piping and electrical wiring needed to be fixed, but overall, the home has a strong foundation.

That's how the duplex will be from now on too—less to fix, easier to restore, with a strong foundation to build on, and a safe place to embrace people. We are like that house. When the unhealthy patterns have been broken, healing becomes easier to maintain and people become easier to welcome in. To break the patterns, I encourage you to invite others in to see the new foundation you've built. And remember that every unhealthy pattern you break, every torn-down piece you rebuild, and every step closer to healing you take deserves to be danced over, because it is our healing that increases our capacity for love. Healing increases our capacity to be a safe house.

In the Bible there is an often-overlooked woman named Miriam. Her baby brother was at risk of being murdered due to a ruler's decree to kill all the Hebrew male newborn babies. To protect her son, Miriam's mom hid him in a basket and put him in a river. Miriam kept a close watch over her brother, and when the pharaoh's daughter discovered the boy in the basket, Miriam asked if she wanted a Hebrew woman to nurse him. When the pharaoh's daughter agreed, Miriam went to her mom, who was then able to return to the baby and care for him. Through her watchfulness, Miriam became a safe house and saved her brother. This baby, whom we later know as Moses, delivered the Israelite people from slavery. He was one of the greatest and most important leaders and prophets in history. Every hero needs a safe house like Miriam.

Miriam, Moses, and their other brother, Aaron, led the people of Israel from slavery to the promised land after miraculously crossing the Red Sea on dry ground and seeing the Egyptian army overthrown into the sea. After much adversity, Miriam grabbed a tambourine and led the women to worship God with song and dance. She was then given the title *prophetess*, the first of only a handful of women in Scripture identified that way. Miriam's dancing led to others' dancing, just as our freedom can lead others into their own freedom.

Jeremiah 31:3–4 says,

The LORD appeared to us in the past, saying:

> "I have loved you with an everlasting love;
>> I have drawn you with unfailing kindness.
> I will build you up again,
>> and you, Virgin Israel, will be rebuilt.
> Again you will take up your timbrels
>> and go out to dance with the joyful.

May this season mark your freedom and restoration and spur you on to dance. And if your response is, "I don't know how to dance," I say that's not true. The reality is, we all know how to dance. We are just worried about what others will think if we bust a move. Dancing is the bodily epitome of human freedom. We all have it within us. Dancing, loving, healing are the same in this way: We just need to know the voice of God to do them well.

PATTERNS TO BREAK AND TRUTHS TO EMBRACE

CHANGING OUR PATTERNS DOES NOT HAPPEN IN A single instant. It takes time. When those times seem really hard, when your thought patterns loop and spiral unexpectedly, take a look at this simple chart I created for you. Take a few moments to write in the patterns you want to break and the truths you need to embrace. I already added the ones we've discussed in the book—along with a few extras—so you can always have them to refer to.

THOUGHT PATTERN TO BREAK	TRUTH TO EMBRACE
There is something wrong with me.	There is something right with me.
Seeking help and crying are signs of weakness.	Seeking help is brave and necessary. Crying is a sign of strength and healing.
I have no reason to like or love myself.	I have permission to love who God has created me to be. God did a good job making me.
I am a victim.	I am a victor, and sometimes I must step out of my own means of self-destructing to see who I am created to be.
I need to love like I've never been hurt.	Love is awake to the pain it has endured. My suffering and hurt will never be wasted. When we acknowledge, process, and heal our pain, we become more equipped to love others the way they need to be loved. We must love like we have been hurt to love with compassion and empathy. My hurt can transform to help.

THOUGHT PATTERN TO BREAK	TRUTH TO EMBRACE
My pain and my mistakes have disqualified me.	The pain I have been through and the mistakes I have made make me better able to relate to others in their pain and mistakes. My hurt, when understood, is possibly my greatest asset when loving those around me.
The best leaders are poised and perfect.	The best leaders are vulnerable and honest. The best leaders do not function like miniature gods but humble people.
Humility is making myself smaller so others will be comfortable.	As my mentor Danielle Strickland says, "Humility is simply agreeing with who God says you are." I agree with God that I am nothing more or nothing less than who he says I am. If I am unsure, I can seek wise counsel and look to Scripture, which God has given me to know.

THOUGHT PATTERN TO BREAK	TRUTH TO EMBRACE
Embracing my gifts makes me egocentric and prideful.	Embracing the gifts God has given me is glorifying and honoring to the one who gave me those gifts.
I have to be perfect to step into my calling or do meaningful work that helps others.	We become more like Jesus when we step into what he has called us to. We embrace the process to become holy when we embrace our vocation as love.
This is simply who I am. I cannot change it.	Some patterns must be addressed. Jesus is safe, and I can address my patterns with him.
I will always be like this because of what they did to me.	They are responsible for their actions, but I am responsible for myself and my own healing. I can control myself and myself only.
I am so messed up I will never be completely healed.	I accept that I likely will not experience complete healing on earth, but I joyfully await the day I am eye to eye with my Father in heaven. Until then, all God is and all he has done for me is enough. I will boldly dance and shamelessly cry unto the Lord. After all, I am only human.

THOUGHT PATTERN TO BREAK	TRUTH TO EMBRACE
I am not doing well because my faith is not strong enough.	I can have an authentic faith and a deep relationship with Jesus and still struggle. Suffering is not a measure of faith. My true heart is seen and understood by God, who loves me so.
Time will heal me.	What I do with my time will bring healing. God grants me wisdom and discernment on how to heal. God's love will heal me.
I am incapable of having healthy relationships.	I may need to step back and take a look at my own patterns. I may need to take some responsibility for a dependency that has been placed on other means besides God, but I was made for connectedness.
Dance like no one's watching.	I will dance like I am dancing unto the Lord because I know his opinion of me. His opinion of me is good, and it trumps every other opinion. I will not be dependent on the voices of others because I know the voice of God.

THOUGHT PATTERN TO BREAK	TRUTH TO EMBRACE
Love stays forever.	Love discerns when to remain in relationships and when to leave relationships that have become dysfunctional, unhealthy, and toxic.
I am the labels they placed upon me.	I am who God says I am. Loved. Created with a purpose. Cherished.
I don't belong there.	I belong right where I am
I'm the problem. Or I am a "prodigal."	I am not a problem or a prodigal child. There will always be tension when change starts. I am breaking patterns that need to be broken.
I need closure.	I do not need an apology or resolution from any person because God knows it all. What is true will all be revealed in his perfect timing. I may need to forgive or apologize to receive forgiveness.

ACKNOWLEDGMENTS

THE UNWAVERING SACRIFICE OF JACOB, MY HUSBAND, is the backbone of this book and ministry. You are a rock. When life gets hard I hear your voice whisper, "You have to do it." You propel me toward Christ. I am much more of who God created me to be because I have you, my partner.

To my children, you are the reason I heal. These words wouldn't be written without the miraculous motivation you possess by simply existing.

Tonya, there will never be enough words to adequately praise you for all you have done for me. If I wasn't striving to look like Jesus, I would strive to look like you, because I think you're the closest reflection of him that I have ever seen embodied. I am a safe house to some because you have been a safe house to many. Your hospitality will forever inspire mine.

Scott, you loved me when I did not know how to accept love. You chased me when I chased other families, believing for better. But with you, I know now I have always had the best.

To my church leadership, especially Pastor Tim, Andy,

Ruth, Shawn, and Ashlee, because of your steadfast love and leadership, I am able to love and lead unhindered. I will be indebted to you for the rest of my life. Thank you for welcoming me back home as if I never left. You've seen what God was doing in me so clearly before I ever even caught a glimpse. I stand on the shoulders of you all, the most humble giants.

I write this book after my first year of seminary, and I'm not sure if I'll make it through to graduate, but to the women in my cohort, you have kept me leaning into Jesus' Word. This book is deeper and richer, with more of God's Word, because of how you have held me and what we have learned together.

Zoe, I am more thoughtful because of your thoughtfulness. Your accountability has helped me to delight in reading Scripture and praying. Our friendship is a treasure to me.

The enthusiastic support of Bob Goff is what caused me to continue in this ministry when I felt like giving up. God sent you as a friend in my life to cheer me on with confetti, balloons, and high praises. When I could not think much of myself, you made much of me.

Danielle Strickland, thank you for being among the first to see my potential. I am so fortunate to have you as a mentor in my life who I can approach with the most unfiltered questions. You guide me with grace. You call me up with such love and boldness. I love more like Christ and more boldly because of your love for me.

To Kimberly, my hurricane of a sister in Christ. For the longest time you were the loudest voice in my head. Now you are forever silent. There will always be a seat for you, but I will never allow you a microphone again. I love who you have helped me become.

To Andy, who said, "Do not become another typical Christian self-help author." I didn't know what you meant by that until I started writing. Those were the words that compelled me to hold nothing back. I am holding on to my anger the best way I know how.

To Thomas Nelson and Austin, thank you for believing in the message between these pages. I think a lot about how some voices in leadership believe young people need to wait until they're more refined and complete to do work like write a book. While I understand the well-meaning intention, I wonder who is meeting those coming into the faith, with all their brokenness, nose-to-nose, rather than with a pointed finger. Because of you, it is us. We will meet the hurting ones through these pages. We will not leave anyone in the mucky middle behind.

I love you all.

To God be the glory forever and ever, for anything good in me is him.

NOTES

LIE 1: SELF-LOVE IS SELFISH
1. Genesis 1:31.
2. Mark 12:28–31.
3. Genesis 1:27–31.

LIE 2: LOVE LIKE YOU'VE NEVER BEEN HURT
1. *Merriam-Webster*, s.v. "despise (*v.*)," accessed June 1, 2024, https://www.merriam-webster.com/thesaurus/despise.
2. Matthew 26:26.
3. Luke 22:19 NLT.

LIE 3: TO LOVE IS TO BE VULNERABLE, ALWAYS
1. Proverbs 4:20–21.
2. C. S. Lewis, *The Four Loves* (Harcourt Brace, 1960), 121.
3. Marina Berzins McCoy, *Wounded Heroes: Vulnerability as a Virtue in Ancient Greek Literature and Philosophy* (Oxford University Press, 2013), vii.

LIE 4: SOMEDAY IS BETTER THAN TODAY
1. "High Education for Foster Youth," National Foster Youth Institute, accessed October 3, 2025, https://nfyi.org/issues /higher-education/.
2. Esther 4:14.

LIE 5: TIME HEALS ALL WOUNDS

1. "People Who Were Abused as Children Are More Likely To Be Abused as an Adult," Office for National Statistics, September 27, 2017, https://www.ons.gov.uk /peoplepopulationandcommunity/crimeandjustice/articles /peoplewhowereabusedaschildrenaremorelikelytobeabusedasanadult /2017-09-27.
2. Krystina Murray, "Broken Homes and Spirits: Examining Childhood Adversity," Addiction Center, August 27, 2020, https://www.addictioncenter.com/news/2020/08 /examining-early-childhood-adversity.
3. Maria Otero, "Six Kilometers a Day," United States Agency for International Development, accessed June 4, 2024, https://www.usaid.gov/six-kilometers-day.
4. John 4:29, paraphrased.
5. Matthew 18:12–13.

LIE 6: YOUR FEELINGS ARE NOT VALID

1. Hebrews 12:1–3.
2. "Codependency," Mental Health America, accessed June 4, 2024, https://www.mhanational.org/co-dependency.
3. Proverbs 19:20; Romans 13:5; Jeremiah 17:9.
4. For example, see the New American Standard Bible and King James Version translations of 2 Timothy 3:6–7.
5. *Englishman's Concordance*, s.v. "γυμνὰ (gymna)," Bible Hub, accessed June 4, 2024, https://biblehub.com/greek /gumna_1131.htm.

LIE 7: YOU HAVE TO DEFEND YOURSELF

1. Norman B. Schmidt et al., "Exploring Human Freeze Responses to a Threat Stressor," *Journal of Behavior Therapy and Experimental Psychiatry* 39, no. 3 (2008): 292–304, https://doi.org/10.1016/j.jbtep.2007.08.002.

2. "Always on Alert: Causes and Examples of Hypervigilance," Cleveland Clinic, November 15, 2023, https://health .clevelandclinic.org/hypervigilance.

3. Pete Walker, *Complex PTSD: From Surviving to Thriving* (Azure Coyote, 2021).

4. Luke 9:23; 1 Corinthians 10:24.

5. Valerie Fentress, "How Old Was David When He Killed Goliath?" Christianity.com, March 19, 2024, https://www .christianity.com/wiki/bible/how-old-was-david-when-he -killed-goliath.html.

6. 1 Samuel 17:37.

LIE 8: THERE IS SOMETHING WRONG WITH YOU

1. Arthur J. Droge, "Did Paul Commit Suicide?" *Bible Review* 5, no. 6 (1989): https://library.biblicalarchaeology.org /article/did-paul-commit-suicide/.

2. Tina Fossella, "Human Nature, Buddha Nature: On Spiritual Bypassing, Relationship, and the Dharma," *Tricycle Magazine* (2011), archived at http://www.johnwelwood.com/articles /TRIC_interview_uncut.pdf.

3. Revelation 2:17.

4. Brennan Manning, *The Furious Longing of God* (David C. Cook, 2009), 46.

5. 1 Kings 19:9–13 ESV.

6. John 10:10.

LIE 9: YOU'RE A BABY CHRISTIAN, SO YOUR FAITH IS IMMATURE

1. Proverbs 18:21.

2. Matthew 9:36.

3. Matthew 5:3–12.

4. Matthew 18:1–5.

5. 2 Kings 5:1–14.

LIE 10: YOU CAN'T CHANGE YOUR STORY

1. "Housing and Homelessness," National Foster Youth Institute, accessed October 3, 2024, https://nfyi.org/issues/homelessness/.
2. "Cognitive Dissonance," *Psychology Today*, accessed June 8, 2024, https://www.psychologytoday.com/us/basics/cognitive-dissonance.
3. "The 4 Attachment Styles and How They Impact You," Cleveland Clinic, September 22, 2022, https://health.clevelandclinic.org/attachment-theory-and-attachment-styles.

LIE 11: YOU HAVE TO FIGURE OUT YOUR CALLING

1. Martin G. Collins, "You Are My Witnesses," *Forerunner*, Church of the Great God, December 1997, https://www.cgg.org/index.cfm/library/article/id/310/you-are-my-witnesses.htm.
2. Matthew 25:40.
3. John 13:35.
4. Song of Songs 2:10–11, 13–15 TPT.

LIE 12: TO LOVE MEANS TO STAY, NO MATTER WHAT

1. Joel 2:25.
2. Luke 5:15–16.
3. John 6:25–66.
4. "'You do not want to leave too, do you?' Jesus asked the Twelve" (John 6:67).

LIE 13: YOU'RE NOT READY YET

1. Galatians 1:24.
2. Romans 12:3–8 ESV.
3. 2 Corinthians 11:5–6 CSB.
4. "Child Welfare and Foster Care Statistics," Annie E. Casey Foundation, May 16, 2022, https://www.aecf.org/blog/child-welfare-and-foster-care-statistics.

5. Mohsin Modi ud Din, "How Connecting Neuroscience, Storytelling, and Psychology Can Create Measurable Impact for Refugee Youth," UN Refugee Agency, accessed June 6, 2024, https://www.unhcr.org/innovation/connecting-neuroscience -storytelling-psychology-can-create-measurable-impact-refugee -youth.
6. Mark 5:1–20 NLT.
7. Mark 1:43–44 ESV.
8. James 1:27.

LIE 14: YOU NEED CLOSURE TO HEAL
1. Romans 12:17–21 ESV.
2. Psalm 23:5.

TRUTH: YOU ARE A PATTERN BREAKER
1. Bella Smith, "Avoiding Your Triggers Is Not Healing," Psych Times Publication, August 29, 2023, https:// psychtimespublication.com /avoiding-your-triggers-is-not-healing-e87dd2d7aa78.
2. Leo Newhouse, "Is Crying Good for You?," *Harvard Health Blog*, March 1, 2021, https://www.health.harvard.edu/blog /is-crying-good-for-you-2021030122020.
3. Hannah John, "British Science Festival: 7 Ways Dancing Can Improve Your Life," British Science Association, September 25, 2019, https://www.britishscienceassociation.org/blogs /bsa-blog/7-ways-dancing-can-improve-your-life.
4. 2 Samuel 6:14 NLT.
5. 2 Samuel 6:15.

ABOUT THE AUTHOR

TORI HOPE PETERSEN IS AN AUTHOR, SPEAKER, BIBLE teacher, and lover of people. Since coming to faith, she has shared her testimony and life as authentically as she can to help and offer hope to others. Tori is known for her fierce advocacy work for foster care, adoption, and vulnerable children. At home she is a wife and mama who enjoys cooking with her children. With a deep value for family, community, and hospitality, Tori and her family love to make extra food for whoever might stop by.

Would you like to purchase multiple copies of

BREAKING THE PATTERNS THAT BREAK YOU

for a book club or small group?

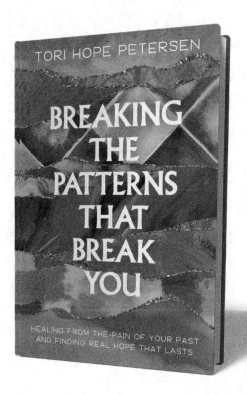

Scan the QR code

to learn more.

NOTES

NOTES

NOTES

NOTES

_____

_____

_____

_____

_____

_____

_____

_____

_____

_____

_____

_____

_____

_____

_____

_____

_____

NOTES

_____

_____

_____

_____

_____

_____

_____

_____

_____

_____

_____

_____

_____

_____

_____

_____

_____

_____

NOTES